MANIFEST MIRACLES

ATTRACT MIRACLES AND ABUNDANCE WITH THE POWER OF MANIFESTATION

TUSHAR MEGHANI

Made with ❤ on the Notion Press Platform
www.notionpress.com

I dedicate this book with deep gratitude and appreciation to my parents, who have always been my pillars of strength and have supported me in every step of my life. To my uncle and aunt, who have been like second parents to me and have taught me the value of kindness and compassion. To my younger brother, Diven, who always inspires me with his enthusiasm and energy.

To my late Dada and nani, who may not be with us physically but have left a lasting impact on my life with their love and wisdom. I know they would be proud of my achievements.

I also want to express my heartfelt gratitude to Jignesh Panseriya, a great mentor who introduced me to the world of the Law of Attraction in his online sessions, "Believe in Yourself". His guidance has been invaluable in shaping my understanding of manifestation.

To all my family members, friends, teachers, and everyone who has played a vital role in my growth and development, I offer my sincere thanks. Your love, support, and encouragement have been instrumental in making me the person I am today. This book is dedicated to each and every one of you.

Contents

Contents

Preface

Welcome to "Manifest Miracles: Attract Miracles And Abundancewith The Power Of Manifestation " This book is your ultimate guide to unlocking the full potential of the Law of Attraction and manifesting the life of your dreams.

If you're reading this, chances are you're already familiar with the Law of Attraction and its potential to transform your life. But maybe you're struggling to put it into practice, or you're not seeing the results you desire. That's where this book comes in.

In these pages, we'll take a deep dive into the principles of the Law of Attraction and how to apply them in your daily life. We'll explore various techniques and strategies for manifestation, including mindfulness, visualization, energy work, and more. You'll learn how to identify and overcome limiting beliefs, cultivate a positive mindset, and align your thoughts and actions with your desires.

I wrote this book with the intention of helping you unlock the power of the Law of Attraction and manifest miracles in your own life. It's my hope that by the end of this book, you'll have the knowledge, tools, and confidence to create the life you truly desire.

So, get ready to experience the magic of manifestation and attract miracles into your life. Let's begin!

Acknowledgements

This book would not have been possible without the support and encouragement of so many people, and I am incredibly grateful for each and every one of them.

First and foremost, I want to express my deepest gratitude to my family for their unwavering love and support. They have always believed in me and encouraged me to follow my dreams, even when they seemed impossible.

I also want to thank my mentor Jignesh Panseriya, who introduced me to the incredible world of the Law of Attraction and helped me to develop my skills in manifestation. His guidance and wisdom have been invaluable.

To my friends and colleagues who have supported me along the way, thank you for your encouragement and belief in me. Your kind words and feedback have been instrumental in shaping this book.

I would also like to thank my readers, who have inspired me to write this book and share my knowledge with the world. Your support and enthusiasm mean everything to me.

Finally, I want to acknowledge all of the teachers, authors, and experts who have contributed to the field of manifestation and the Law of Attraction. Your work has been a constant source of inspiration and guidance for me.

Thank you all for being a part of this journey with me.

With love and gratitude,

Tushar

Acknowledgments

This book would not have been possible without the support and encouragement of so many people, and I am incredibly grateful to each and every one of them.

CHAPTER I

Introduction to the Law of Attraction: The Basics and How it Works

Have you ever wanted to achieve something in your life but felt like you were just spinning your wheels? What if I told you that there's a powerful force you can tap into that can help you manifest your deepest desires and transform your life? That force is known as the Law of Attraction. In this chapter, we'll explore the basics of the Law of Attraction, how it works, and what you can do to start harnessing its power in your life. Whether you're looking to attract more abundance, love, success, or simply improve your overall well-being, the Law of Attraction can help you achieve your goals. But what exactly is the Law of Attraction? In a nutshell, it's the principle that like attracts like. This means that the thoughts and emotions you put out into the universe attract similar experiences and circumstances back to you. For example, if you focus on lack and scarcity, you may attract more experiences of lack and scarcity into your life. Conversely, if you focus on abundance and gratitude, you'll attract more experiences of abundance and gratitude. The Law of Attraction is a concept that has been around for centuries, but it gained popularity in the 20th century through the work of authors such as Napoleon Hill, Norman Vincent Peale, and Dale Carnegie. Today, the Law of Attraction is widely recognized as a powerful tool for personal transformation and manifestation.

What is the Law of Attraction?

The Law of Attraction is a universal principle that states that like attracts like. It's based on the idea that everything in the universe is made up of energy, and that energy vibrates at different frequencies. When you focus your thoughts and emotions on a particular outcome, you send out a vibration that attracts similar frequencies back to you.

To put it simply, the Law of Attraction means that you get what you focus on. If you focus on negative thoughts and emotions, you'll attract negative experiences into your life. Conversely, if you focus on positive thoughts and emotions, you'll attract positive experiences into your life.

The Law of Attraction has been around for centuries, and it's been used by many cultures and religions throughout history. However, it gained popularity in the modern era through the work of authors such as Napoleon Hill, Norman Vincent Peale, and Esther Hicks.

One of the earliest recorded mentions of the Law of Attraction can be found in the ancient Hindu text, the Upanishads. The Upanishads teach that "you are what your deepest desire is," and that "your thoughts become your words, your words become your actions, your actions become your habits, your habits become your character, and your character becomes your destiny."

In the 20th century, the Law of Attraction gained popularity through the work of Napoleon Hill, who wrote the classic book "Think and Grow Rich." Hill believed that the Law of Attraction could be used to achieve wealth, success, and happiness.

Since then, the Law of Attraction has continued to evolve and be popularized by authors and speakers such as Louise Hay, Wayne Dyer, and Esther Hicks. Today, it's widely recognized as a powerful tool for personal transformation and manifestation.

Understanding the Law of Attraction is the first step towards using it to create the life you desire. In the following sections, we'll dive deeper into how the Law of Attraction works and how you can start using it in your daily life. So, if you're ready to learn more about this powerful principle, let's continue!

How Does the Law of Attraction Work?

The Law of Attraction works based on several underlying principles. These principles include the power of thought, the energy of emotions, and the importance of belief.

First, the Law of Attraction is based on the power of thought. Your thoughts have the power to shape your reality, as they influence the way you perceive and interact with the world around you. When you focus your thoughts on a particular outcome, you send out a vibration that attracts similar frequencies back to you.

Second, the Law of Attraction is based on the energy of emotions. Emotions are a powerful form of energy that can either attract or repel the experiences you want in your life. When you feel positive emotions such as joy, gratitude, and love, you send out a vibration that attracts positive experiences back to you. Conversely, when you feel negative emotions such as fear, anger, and sadness, you send out a vibration that attracts negative experiences back to you.

Finally, the Law of Attraction is based on the importance of belief. Your beliefs shape your reality, as they influence the way you interpret and respond to the world around you. When you believe that something is possible, you're more likely to take action towards achieving it. Conversely, when you believe that something is impossible, you're less likely to take action towards achieving it.

The science behind the Law of Attraction is rooted in quantum physics. According to quantum physics, everything in the universe is made up of energy, including our thoughts and emotions. This energy vibrates at different frequencies, and the Law of Attraction states that we attract experiences that match the frequency of our thoughts and emotions.

For example, if you're constantly thinking about how much you hate your job, you're sending out a vibration that attracts more negative experiences related to your job. You may experience more stressful situations at work, or you may have difficulty finding a new job that you enjoy. On the other hand, if you focus on positive thoughts and emotions related to your job, you're more likely to attract positive experiences such as a promotion or a new opportunity.

Key Elements of the Law of Attraction

The Law of Attraction is not just about positive thinking or wishing for something to come true. There are specific elements that are essential to its practice and success:

Thoughts and beliefs: Our thoughts and beliefs create the foundation for our manifestations. If we hold onto negative or limiting beliefs, we will attract negative or limiting experiences. Conversely, if we adopt positive and empowering beliefs, we will attract positive and empowering experiences.

For example, if someone believes that they are not good enough to succeed in their career, they may struggle to advance and find fulfilling opportunities. But if they shift their belief to one of confidence and self-worth, they are more likely to attract opportunities that align with their goals.

Emotions: Our emotions serve as indicators of our alignment or misalignment with our desires. When we feel positive emotions like joy, excitement, and gratitude, we are in alignment with our desires and are more likely to attract them. Negative emotions like fear, doubt, and frustration signal that we are out of alignment and may be blocking our manifestations.

For example, if someone wants to attract a loving relationship, but they constantly feel anxious and doubtful about their ability to find a partner, they may struggle to attract the relationship they desire.

Visualization and imagination: These are powerful tools for manifestation, allowing us to create a clear and vivid mental image of our desired outcome. By using our imagination to visualize ourselves already experiencing our desired outcome, we can attract it more easily.

For example, if someone wants to attract financial abundance, they might visualize themselves with a bank account full of money, feeling secure and free to do the things they love.

Inspired action: While positive thoughts and visualization are important, they must be combined with inspired action to manifest our desires. Inspired action is action that feels good and aligned with our desires, rather than forced or driven by fear or obligation.

For example, if someone wants to attract a new career opportunity, they might start networking with people in their desired field or taking courses to develop new skills.

Gratitude and appreciation: Expressing gratitude and appreciation for what we already have is a key element of the Law of Attraction. When we focus on what we're grateful for, we attract more experiences to be grateful for.

For example, if someone is grateful for their supportive friends and family, they are more likely to attract more positive relationships into their life.

By incorporating these key elements into our practice of the Law of Attraction, we can more effectively manifest our desires and create the life we truly want.

Common Misconceptions about the Law of Attraction

- The Law of Attraction is a magical, instant solution to all problems
- The Law of Attraction requires no action or effort on your part
- The Law of Attraction is just wishful thinking or daydreaming
- The Law of Attraction can manifest negative or harmful situations
- The Law of Attraction only works for certain people

Addressing these common misunderstandings and clarifying the role of action in manifestation is important to avoid confusion and disappointment. While the Law of Attraction can bring opportunities and experiences into your life, it still requires action and effort on your part to achieve your goals. The Law of Attraction can also manifest negative situations if you focus on negative thoughts and emotions. It's important to understand that the Law of Attraction is not a quick fix, but rather a mindset and lifestyle that can lead to long-term positive changes in your life.

Benefits of Practicing the Law of Attraction

- Practicing the Law of Attraction can bring a multitude of benefits to one's life, including improved mental and emotional well-being, enhanced relationships, and increased abundance and success.

- By focusing on positive thoughts and emotions, the Law of Attraction can help individuals cultivate a more optimistic and resilient outlook on life, leading to a decrease in stress and anxiety.
- The Law of Attraction can also improve relationships by promoting greater empathy, understanding, and appreciation for others, and by attracting positive and harmonious interactions.
- Additionally, the Law of Attraction can help individuals achieve greater abundance and success in their lives, whether it be in their career, finances, or personal pursuits, by aligning their thoughts, beliefs, and actions with their desired outcomes.

Overall, the Law of Attraction can enhance one's life in numerous ways, creating a more fulfilling and satisfying existence.

In conclusion, the Law of Attraction is a powerful concept that can have a significant impact on our lives. By understanding and applying its principles, we can manifest our desires and create a more fulfilling life. In this chapter, we have covered the definition and historical background of the Law of Attraction, how it works, the key elements for successful manifestation, and common misconceptions. Additionally, we have discussed the potential benefits of practicing the Law of Attraction and how it can enhance one's life.

It is important to note that while the Law of Attraction can be a transformative practice, it requires effort and commitment to make it work. By incorporating it into our daily lives and continuously aligning our thoughts, beliefs, and actions with our desired outcomes, we can experience positive changes. I encourage readers to continue exploring this concept and discover how the Law of Attraction can benefit them personally.

CHAPTER II

Understanding Your Thoughts and Beliefs: The Foundation of the Law of Attraction

Welcome to the chapter on "Understanding Your Thoughts and Beliefs: The Foundation of the Law of Attraction." In this chapter, we will explore the essential role of thoughts and beliefs in the Law of Attraction and how they influence our experiences and manifestations.

The Law of Attraction operates on the principle that we attract into our lives what we focus on, believe in, and expect. This means that our thoughts and beliefs shape our reality and determine what we manifest. Understanding how to manage and direct our thoughts and beliefs is critical to achieving our desires and creating a fulfilling life.

To gain a comprehensive understanding of the Law of Attraction, we must start with its foundational element, which is our thoughts and beliefs. In this chapter, we will discuss the following topics:

- The power of thoughts and beliefs
- Types of thoughts and beliefs
- Identifying limiting beliefs
- Affirmations and positive self-talk

By the end of this chapter, you will have a deeper understanding of the critical role of thoughts and beliefs in the Law of Attraction and how you can harness their power to achieve your goals and dreams. So, let's get started!

The Power of Thoughts and Beliefs

Our thoughts and beliefs are like a filter that colors our perception of the world around us. They can either serve as a powerful tool for manifestation or as a barrier that blocks us from achieving our desires. The Law of Attraction states that what we focus on expands, and our thoughts and beliefs play a significant role in determining what we focus on.

For instance, if we have a belief that we are not good enough, we may find ourselves feeling inadequate and unworthy of success, which can prevent us from taking the necessary actions to achieve our goals. On the other hand, if we have a positive belief that we are capable and deserving of success, we are more likely to feel confident and take inspired action towards our desired outcomes.

Our thoughts and beliefs also have a direct impact on our emotions and actions. For example, if we think positively about a situation, we are likely to feel positive emotions such as joy, gratitude, and contentment, which can motivate us to take positive actions. In contrast, if we have negative thoughts about a situation, we are likely to experience negative emotions such as fear, anxiety, and sadness, which can hold us back from taking action.

Therefore, it is essential to become aware of our thoughts and beliefs and examine whether they are supporting or hindering our manifestation efforts. By cultivating positive thoughts and beliefs, we can attract positive outcomes and experiences into our lives.

Identifying Limiting Beliefs

Limiting beliefs are thoughts or beliefs that hold us back from achieving our desired outcomes. They are often deeply ingrained and may have been formed from past experiences or societal conditioning. It is important to identify and address these beliefs in order to move towards a more positive and fulfilling life.

To recognize and identify limiting beliefs, start by paying attention to your inner dialogue and the stories you tell yourself. Notice any recurring negative thoughts or self-talk, such as "I‘m not good enough" or "I don’t deserve success." These are often indicators of underlying limiting beliefs.

Another way to identify limiting beliefs is to examine areas of your life where you feel stuck or blocked. Ask yourself what beliefs or thoughts may be contributing to these feelings. For example, if you feel stuck in your career, you may hold a limiting belief that you are not qualified or skilled enough to pursue your dream job.

Common limiting beliefs include:

- "I’m not smart/talented/creative enough."
- "I don’t have enough money/resources/time."
- "Success is only for a lucky few."
- "I don’t deserve to be happy/fulfilled/successful."

By identifying these limiting beliefs, you can start to challenge and replace them with more positive and empowering thoughts. This process can take time and effort, but it is an important step towards creating the life you desire.

Cultivating Positive Thoughts and Beliefs

Cultivating positive thoughts and beliefs is an important step in utilizing the Law of Attraction. By shifting your mindset towards positivity, you can attract more abundance, success, and happiness into your life. Here are some techniques to help you develop a positive mindset:

- Gratitude: Practicing gratitude can help you focus on the positive aspects of your life, rather than the negative. Take time each day to reflect on the things you are grateful for, whether it be your health, loved ones, or simply a beautiful sunset.
- Positive Self-Talk: Monitor your self-talk and make a conscious effort to reframe negative thoughts into positive ones. For example, instead of thinking "I can't do this," try thinking "I am capable and will figure it out."
- Visualization: Visualization is a powerful tool for manifesting your desires. Spend time visualizing your goals and dreams as if they have already come true. This can help you attract the experiences and opportunities that will lead to your desired outcome.
- Affirmations: Affirmations are positive statements that can help you reinforce positive beliefs. Repeat affirmations to yourself daily, such as "I am worthy of success and abundance" or "I am confident and capable."

By incorporating these techniques into your daily routine, you can train your mind to focus on the positive and cultivate a mindset of abundance and success.

The Law of Attraction in Action

The Law of Attraction is a powerful tool that can manifest our desires and help us achieve our goals. One of the most important aspects of the Law of Attraction is the power of our thoughts and beliefs. Our thoughts and beliefs can either attract or repel the things we want in life.

In this chapter, we will explore real-life examples of how thoughts and beliefs have manifested in people's lives. We will also discuss how to use the power of thoughts and beliefs to manifest desired outcomes.

Real-Life Examples

There are countless examples of how the Law of Attraction has worked in people's lives. Here are a few real-life examples:

- A woman who wanted to find a romantic partner. She visualized herself in a happy, loving relationship and wrote down all the qualities she wanted in a partner. Within a few months, she met her ideal partner and they have been happily together ever since.
- An entrepreneur who wanted to start his own business. He visualized himself as a successful business owner and believed in his abilities. He took action to start his business and it quickly grew into a successful company.

Using Thoughts and Beliefs to Manifest Desired Outcomes

To use the power of thoughts and beliefs to manifest desired outcomes, it's important to follow these steps:

1. Identify your desires: What do you want to achieve or attract into your life?
2. Visualize: Create a clear mental image of what you want. Imagine yourself already having achieved it and feel the emotions associated with it.
3. Believe: Believe that your desire is already on its way to you. Trust the universe and yourself.
4. Take action: Take inspired action towards your desire. This means taking actions that align with your desire and staying open to new opportunities.
5. Gratitude: Practice gratitude for what you already have and what is on its way to you. Gratitude helps to reinforce positive thoughts and beliefs.

By following these steps and using the power of your thoughts and beliefs, you can manifest your desired outcomes and achieve your goals.

Common Challenges and Pitfalls

Changing thoughts and beliefs can be a challenging process. It's important to be aware of potential obstacles that can arise and strategies for overcoming them.

- Resistance: Resistance is a common obstacle that can arise when trying to change limiting beliefs. This resistance can manifest as procrastination, self-doubt, or even fear of success. One strategy for overcoming resistance is to focus on the benefits of the new belief and to take small, manageable steps towards implementing it.
- Negative self-talk: Negative self-talk can be a major obstacle to changing limiting beliefs. This can include thoughts like "I'm not good enough" or "I can't do this." To overcome negative self-talk, it's important to replace these thoughts with positive affirmations and to focus on progress rather than perfection.
- Lack of consistency: Changing thoughts and beliefs takes consistent effort over time. It's important to make a commitment to daily practices like positive affirmations and visualization to reinforce positive beliefs.
- External influences: External influences like negative people or situations can also be a challenge to maintaining positive beliefs. One strategy for overcoming external influences is to surround yourself with positive people and to limit exposure to negative influences as much as possible.

By being aware of these potential challenges and pitfalls, it's possible to stay aligned with positive thoughts and beliefs and to manifest desired outcomes in life.

In conclusion, this chapter has explored the importance of thoughts and beliefs in the Law of Attraction. We learned how our thoughts and beliefs shape our reality and affect our emotions and actions. It is essential to recognize and identify our limiting beliefs, as they can hinder our manifestation efforts. Overcoming limiting beliefs requires strategies such as positive affirmations and self-talk.

Cultivating positive thoughts and beliefs is also crucial to manifesting our desires successfully. Techniques like visualization and affirmations can help us develop a positive mindset and reinforce our positive beliefs. However, there can be challenges and obstacles along the way, such as negative self-talk or doubts.

To overcome these challenges, we must stay aligned with our positive beliefs and practice self-awareness. It is essential to stay focused on our goals and desires to manifest them successfully. Identifying our goals and desires can help us achieve a clear focus and stay on track with our manifestation efforts.

Remember, the Law of Attraction works through the power of thoughts and beliefs. By changing our thoughts and beliefs and focusing on what we want, we can manifest our desires into reality. So, start cultivating positive thoughts and beliefs, and watch the magic happen!

CHAPTER III

Identifying Your Goals and Desires: Clarity and Focus in Manifestation

Welcome to the chapter on "Identifying Your Goals and Desires: Clarity and Focus in Manifestation". In this chapter, we will explore the crucial role that goal-setting and desire-identification play in the Law of Attraction. We will discuss how having a clear understanding of your goals and desires can help you to focus your thoughts and energy towards manifesting them into reality. Through practical tips and real-life examples, we will guide you on how to identify your goals and desires to achieve clarity and focus in your manifestation journey. So, let's dive in!

Understanding Your True Desires

When it comes to manifestation, it's important to have a clear understanding of your true desires. Often, we may think we want something because it's what society or our family has told us we should want, or because it's a surface-level desire that we think will make us happy.

However, surface-level desires are often temporary and don't bring lasting fulfillment. It's important to dig deeper and uncover your true, deep desires – the things that truly align with your soul and purpose.

One way to do this is through introspection and self-reflection. Take some time to sit quietly and think about what truly brings you joy and fulfillment, what makes your heart sing, and what you feel passionate about.

Another technique is journaling. Write down your thoughts and feelings about what you want in life and what truly matters to you. This can help you uncover patterns and themes in your desires.

Visualization is also a powerful tool for uncovering your true desires. Imagine yourself living the life you truly want and pay attention to the details – where you are, who you're with, what you're doing. These details can give you clues about what truly matters to you.

It's important to note that your true desires may evolve and change over time, so it's important to regularly check in with yourself and reassess what you truly want. By uncovering your true desires, you can set clear goals and intentions that align with your soul and purpose, making manifestation more effective and fulfilling

Setting Clear and Specific Goals

One of the most crucial steps towards manifestation is setting clear and specific goals. Your goals provide a clear direction and focus on what you want to achieve. The more specific and clear your goals are, the easier it is for the universe to understand what you want to manifest.

The SMART framework is a useful technique for setting effective goals. It stands for Specific, Measurable, Achievable, Relevant, and Time-bound.

- Specific: Be as specific as possible about what you want to achieve. Instead of saying, "I want to be rich," say "I want to earn $1 million by the end of the year."
- Measurable: Set goals that you can measure to track your progress. For example, if you want to lose weight, set a goal to lose 10 pounds in a month.
- Achievable: Make sure your goals are realistic and achievable. Setting unrealistic goals can lead to disappointment and frustration.

- Relevant: Your goals should align with your true desires and be relevant to your life.
- Time-bound: Set a specific deadline for achieving your goals. This creates a sense of urgency and motivation to take action towards your goals.

Example:

Let's say you want to manifest a new job. Instead of simply saying, "I want a new job," you can set a SMART goal by saying, "I want to land a job as a marketing manager in the next three months with a salary of $80,000 or more per year." This goal is specific, measurable, achievable, relevant, and time-bound, making it easier to manifest.

Creating a Vision Board

A vision board is a powerful tool for manifesting your desires. It is essentially a visual representation of your goals and desires, created by cutting out images and words from magazines and other sources and arranging them on a board. Here are some tips for creating an effective vision board:

1. Get Clear on Your Desires: Before you start creating your vision board, it's important to get clear on your desires. Spend some time thinking about what you really want, and write down your goals in detail.
2. Gather Materials: Once you know what you want to manifest, gather materials to create your vision board. This can include magazines, scissors, glue, markers, and any other materials that inspire you.
3. Choose Images and Words: Look through your magazines and other sources for images and words that represent your goals and desires. Choose ones that resonate with you on a deep level.

4. Arrange Your Board: Once you have your images and words, arrange them on your board in a way that feels meaningful and inspiring to you. You can use colors, shapes, and other design elements to make your board visually appealing.
5. Display Your Board: Once your vision board is complete, display it somewhere where you can see it every day. This will help keep your goals and desires at the forefront of your mind, and will help you stay focused on manifesting them.

For example, if your goal is to travel the world, you could include images of exotic destinations, maps, and quotes about travel on your vision board. By looking at your board every day, you will stay motivated and inspired to make your dreams a reality.

Staying Aligned with Your Desires

After identifying your true desires and setting clear and specific goals, it's important to stay focused and motivated on the path to manifestation. Here are some tools and techniques to help you maintain alignment:

- Gratitude Practices: Practicing gratitude helps to shift your focus from what you lack to what you already have. It's a powerful way to raise your vibration and attract more of what you desire. You can start a gratitude journal and write down a few things you're grateful for every day. Alternatively, you can take a few minutes each day to meditate on the things you're grateful for.
- Visualize Your Desired Outcome: Visualization is a powerful technique that helps you to align your thoughts and emotions with your desired outcome. Spend some time each day visualizing yourself already

having achieved your goal. Feel the emotions that come with achieving that goal and let them fill you up.

- Journaling: Journaling can be a powerful way to gain clarity and stay focused on your desires. Write down your goals and desires and reflect on them often. Use your journal to track your progress and celebrate your successes.
- Surround Yourself with Positive Energy: The people you surround yourself with can have a significant impact on your energy and motivation. Seek out like-minded individuals who are also working towards their goals. Join a support group or find an accountability partner to help you stay on track.

By implementing these tools and techniques, you can stay aligned with your desires and remain focused and motivated on your path to manifestation.

Overcoming Obstacles and Roadblocks

Obstacles and roadblocks are a natural part of any journey, including the manifestation process. Some common challenges that can arise include self-doubt, fear, and limiting beliefs.

One strategy for overcoming these challenges is to focus on positive self-talk and affirmations. This can involve repeating empowering phrases to yourself, such as "I am capable and deserving of achieving my goals."

Another effective technique is to practice visualization, where you imagine yourself already having achieved your desired outcome. This can help to reinforce positive beliefs and maintain motivation.

It's also important to stay persistent and committed to your goals, even in the face of setbacks or unexpected obstacles. Remember that every challenge presents an opportunity for growth and learning, and that every step you take brings you closer to your desired outcome.

By staying positive, focused, and committed, you can overcome any obstacles that arise and continue to manifest your dreams and desires.

Celebrating Successes and Manifestations

In the manifestation process, it's important to not only focus on the end goal, but also to celebrate the successes and manifestations that occur along the way. Taking time to acknowledge and appreciate your achievements can help to boost your motivation and confidence, and keep you aligned with your desires.

One technique for celebrating success is to keep a gratitude journal. Write down the things you're grateful for each day, including any progress you've made towards your goals. This can help you stay focused on the positive aspects of your journey and keep you motivated.

Another technique is to create a manifestation scrapbook or vision board, where you can track your progress and visually see the manifestations that have already occurred. This can serve as a reminder of the power of manifestation and help you stay aligned with your desires.

Remember, manifestation is a process and not an overnight success. Celebrating your successes along the way can help to keep you motivated and focused on achieving your ultimate goals.

In conclusion, this chapter emphasized the importance of identifying your goals and desires in the manifestation process. By understanding the difference between surface-level desires and deep desires, setting clear and specific goals, creating a vision board, staying aligned with your desires, overcoming obstacles and celebrating successes, you can achieve your dreams and desires.

It is essential to take action and start identifying your true desires to create a clear focus in manifestation. You can use the techniques and tools provided in this chapter to develop a deeper understanding of yourself and what you truly want in life. Remember, staying positive, persistent, and grateful throughout the manifestation process is key to achieving your goals.

By taking action and staying committed to your desires, you will manifest the life you desire. For example, if your goal is to start a successful business, identify your true desire for starting the business, set specific and clear goals, create a vision board, and stay aligned with your desires through gratitude practices and journaling. With time and persistence, you will celebrate the success of achieving your goals and living the life you desire.

CHAPTER IV

Visualization Techniques: Creating a Clear and Vivid Picture of Your Desired Outcome

Visualization is a powerful tool that can help you manifest your goals and desires. By creating a clear and vivid mental picture of your desired outcome, you can tap into the power of your subconscious mind and attract what you want into your life. In this chapter, we will explore various techniques for visualization and provide you with practical tips to help you make the most out of this powerful manifestation tool. Whether you want to attract more abundance, improve your relationships, or achieve any other goal, visualization can help you manifest your desires. So, let's dive in and discover how to use visualization to create a clear and vivid picture of your desired outcome.

Understanding Visualization

Visualization is a technique that involves creating a mental image or picture of a desired outcome. It works by tapping into the power of the mind to create a clear and vivid picture of what we want to manifest in our lives. Visualization helps us to align our thoughts and beliefs with our desired outcomes, creating a positive and powerful energy that can attract our goals and desires to us.

For example, if you want to manifest a new job, you can visualize yourself in your dream job, working in a beautiful office with friendly colleagues and feeling fulfilled and happy in your work. This visualization can help you to focus your thoughts and beliefs on the positive aspects of your desired outcome, and attract opportunities that will help you to achieve your goal.

The Science of Visualization

In recent years, there has been a growing interest in the science behind visualization, and how it can impact our brain and behavior. Studies have shown that when we visualize a desired outcome, our brain processes that information in a similar way to actually experiencing it. This is because visualization activates the same neural networks that are involved in perception, attention, and action planning.

When we visualize, our brain creates new neural pathways that strengthen the connections between different brain regions. This can improve our ability to remember, learn, and problem-solve, as well as enhance our performance in various tasks. In fact, athletes and performers often use visualization techniques to prepare for competitions and performances, as studies have shown that visualization can lead to improvements in physical and mental performance.

Overall, the science of visualization highlights the power of our thoughts and beliefs, and how they can influence our brain and behavior. By using visualization techniques, we can tap into this power and create a clear and vivid picture of our desired outcomes, which can help to align our thoughts and beliefs with our goals and desires.

Techniques for Effective Visualization

In this chapter, we will explore techniques for effective visualization to help you manifest your desires. Visualizing involves creating a clear and vivid picture of your desired outcome in your mind. Visualization is a powerful tool that can help align your thoughts and beliefs with your desired outcomes, and research has shown that it can have a positive impact on the brain and enhance performance.

To create a successful visualization practice, it is important to follow certain steps. These include finding a quiet and comfortable space, focusing on your breathing to relax your body and mind, and then creating a clear picture of your desired outcome. It is also helpful to incorporate all of your senses and emotions into your visualization to make it more vivid and realistic.

To make your visualizations more effective, you can try techniques such as guided imagery, where you listen to a recorded visualization that guides you through the process, or mental rehearsal, where you mentally practice achieving your desired outcome in a specific situation. It is also important to stay positive and believe in the possibility of your desired outcome.

By incorporating these techniques into your daily routine, you can strengthen your visualization practice and enhance your ability to manifest your desires.

Visualization Exercises

Visualization exercises can be a powerful tool for manifesting your desired outcomes. There are many different types of visualizations that can be tailored to suit your individual goals and preferences. For example, if your goal is to attract abundance, you might visualize yourself surrounded by wealth and abundance in your ideal environment. If your goal is to improve your health, you might visualize yourself feeling strong, healthy, and vibrant.

When designing a visualization exercise, it's important to consider your personal strengths and preferences. Some people are more visual, while others may be more kinesthetic or auditory. Tailoring your visualization to your preferred learning style can help to make it more effective.

Guided visualizations are a popular way to practice visualization. These exercises are typically led by a narrator or coach who guides you through a series of visualizations designed to help you achieve your desired outcome. Guided visualizations can be found online or through various manifestation programs.

It's also important to make your visualizations as vivid and realistic as possible. This means incorporating all of your senses, such as sight, sound, smell, touch, and taste, into your visualization. The more vivid and real your visualization feels, the more likely it is to be effective in manifesting your desired outcome.

Overall, visualization exercises can be a powerful tool for manifesting your desires. By tailoring your visualizations to your personal strengths and preferences, and making them as vivid and realistic as possible, you can enhance their effectiveness and increase your chances of success.

Integrating Visualization into Daily Life

Integrating visualization into your daily life can be a powerful tool for manifesting your desires. Here are some tips for incorporating visualization into your routine:

- Set aside dedicated time for visualization. This could be a few minutes in the morning or before bed, or even during your lunch break.
- Use reminders throughout the day to trigger visualization. For example, you could set an alarm on your phone to remind you to take a few minutes to visualize your desired outcome.
- Incorporate visualization into other daily activities, such as exercise or meditation. For example, while you're

going for a run or doing yoga, visualize yourself achieving your goals.

- Use visualization in conjunction with other manifestation techniques, such as affirmations or gratitude practices. This can help to reinforce positive beliefs and attitudes.

Remember, the key to effective visualization is consistency and repetition. By incorporating visualization into your daily routine, you can help to solidify your desires and increase the likelihood of manifesting them.

Common Challenges and Pitfalls

Integrating visualization into your daily life is crucial for making progress towards your goals and desires. Here are some tips on how to make visualization a habit:

- Start small: Incorporate visualization into your morning or evening routine for just a few minutes each day. Gradually increase the amount of time as you become more comfortable with the practice.
- Make it a daily habit: Consistency is key in developing any habit, so commit to visualizing every day, even if it's just for a few minutes.
- Use reminders: Set reminders on your phone or put up visual cues around your home or office to remind you to take time for visualization.
- Combine with other practices: Visualization can be used in conjunction with other manifestation techniques, such as gratitude practices, affirmations, or goal-setting.
- Be creative: Tailor your visualizations to your personal preferences and strengths. If you're a visual learner, use images and videos to enhance your visualizations. If you're more auditory, incorporate music or guided

meditations.

Remember, the key to effective visualization is to create a clear and vivid picture of your desired outcome, incorporating all of your senses and emotions. With practice and consistency, you can make visualization a powerful tool in your manifestation journey.

In conclusion, visualization is a powerful tool for manifestation that can help align thoughts and beliefs with desired outcomes. By creating a clear and vivid picture of our goals and desires, we can enhance our brain's performance and create a positive mindset that supports our manifestation efforts. This chapter has provided an overview of the science behind visualization, techniques for effective visualization, and guided visualization exercises for specific goals and desires. By integrating visualization into daily routines and habits, and using it in conjunction with other manifestation techniques, we can maximize our manifestation efforts and achieve our goals more easily. We encourage readers to incorporate visualization techniques into their manifestation practice and experience the transformative power of visualization firsthand.

CHAPTER V

Affirmations: Programming Your Subconscious Mind for Success

This chapter will explore the use of affirmations as a powerful tool for manifesting desires. Affirmations are statements that you repeat to yourself, designed to program your subconscious mind with positive beliefs and intentions. The power of affirmations lies in their ability to change your thoughts, feelings, and actions, ultimately leading to the manifestation of your desired outcomes. In this chapter, we will discuss the science behind affirmations, how to create effective affirmations, and strategies for incorporating affirmations into your daily routine. By the end of this chapter, you will have a clear understanding of how to use affirmations to reprogram your subconscious mind for success.

Understanding Affirmations

Affirmations are positive statements that are repeated to oneself in order to program the subconscious mind for success. The power of affirmations lies in their ability to shape our beliefs and behaviors. When we repeat affirmations, we are sending a message to our subconscious mind, which then takes action to bring our thoughts and beliefs into alignment with our desires. For example, if we repeat an affirmation such as "I am confident and successful in all areas of my life," we begin to believe that we are capable of achieving our goals and take actions that lead to success. Affirmations help to create a positive and empowering mindset that supports us in achieving our desires.

The Science of Affirmations

In recent years, there has been growing interest in the science behind affirmations and their effects on the brain and behavior. Research has shown that affirmations can activate the reward centers in the brain, which can boost motivation and positive feelings. Additionally, affirmations can help to reprogram the subconscious mind, which is responsible for our beliefs, habits, and behaviors.

Studies have also found that affirmations can have a positive impact on stress levels and overall well-being. By repeating positive statements to ourselves, we can reduce stress and anxiety and improve our sense of self-efficacy.

One study conducted by researchers at Carnegie Mellon University found that self-affirmations can improve problem-solving abilities and reduce stress responses. Another study published in the journal Personality and Social Psychology Bulletin found that people who regularly used self-affirmations were more likely to achieve their goals and experience positive changes in their lives.

Overall, the science suggests that affirmations can be a powerful tool for enhancing performance, boosting motivation, and improving overall well-being.

Crafting Effective Affirmations

Crafting effective affirmations is essential to the success of the manifestation process. Here are some steps to create affirmations that are specific and impactful:

1. Identify the specific goal or desire: The first step is to identify the specific goal or desire that you want to manifest. This could be related to your career, relationships, health, or any other area of your life.

2. Use positive language: It is important to use positive language in affirmations. Avoid using negative words such as "not" or "never." Instead, focus on what you want to achieve and use positive words to describe it.
3. Keep it simple: Affirmations should be simple and easy to remember. Use short and concise statements that are easy to repeat.
4. Make it personal: Affirmations should be personalized to your specific goals and desires. Use words that resonate with you and make you feel good.
5. Visualize the outcome: As you create your affirmations, visualize yourself achieving your goal or desire. This will help you to create more impactful affirmations that are aligned with your visualization.

For example, if your goal is to improve your self-confidence, you can create an affirmation like "I am confident and capable in everything I do." This affirmation uses positive language and is specific to your goal of improving your self-confidence. You can repeat this affirmation to yourself daily to program your subconscious mind for success.

Using Affirmations for Specific Goals

Using affirmations for specific goals involves crafting affirmations that are aligned with your desired outcome. For example, if you want to manifest abundance, you might use affirmations like "I am attracting abundance into my life" or "Money flows easily and effortlessly to me." For health, you might use affirmations like "I am healthy and vibrant" or "My body is strong and resilient." And for relationships, you might use affirmations like "I am worthy of love and respect" or "I attract loving and supportive relationships into my life."

Tailoring affirmations to personal preferences and strengths involves using language and imagery that resonate with you. For example, if you are a visual person, you might use affirmations that involve mental images or pictures. If you are an auditory person, you might use affirmations that involve sounds or music. And if you are a kinesthetic person, you might use affirmations that involve physical sensations or movements. By tailoring affirmations to your personal preferences and strengths, you can make them more powerful and effective.

Integrating Affirmations into Daily Life

In this section, we will discuss how to integrate affirmations into your daily life to achieve your desired outcomes. This includes incorporating affirmations into your daily routines and habits, such as saying affirmations while brushing your teeth or before bed. We will also explore how affirmations can be used in conjunction with other manifestation techniques, such as visualization and gratitude.

It's important to make affirmations a regular part of your routine so that they become a habit and are more effective. You can write down your affirmations on post-it notes and place them in areas where you will see them frequently, such as on your bathroom mirror or computer screen. This will help you remember to repeat them throughout the day.

Using affirmations in combination with other manifestation techniques can also enhance their effectiveness. For example, you can use visualization techniques to imagine yourself experiencing the reality of your affirmations, and express gratitude for the manifestations you desire as if they have already happened.

Incorporating affirmations into your daily life can help you to stay focused and motivated towards your goals, and can lead to a more positive mindset and increased sense of self-worth.

In conclusion, affirmations can be a powerful tool for manifesting the life you desire. By programming your subconscious mind with positive statements, you can shape your beliefs and behaviors in a way that aligns with your goals. Throughout this chapter, we have discussed the science behind affirmations, how to craft effective affirmations, and how to use them for specific goals. We have also explored ways to integrate affirmations into your daily routine and use them in conjunction with other manifestation techniques.

It's important to remember that affirmations are just one aspect of the manifestation process, but they can be a helpful and empowering addition. By using them consistently and with intention, you can tap into the power of your mind to create the reality you desire. So, I encourage you to start incorporating affirmations into your daily practice and see the positive impact they can have on your life.

CHAPTER VI

Gratitude: Unlocking the Power of Appreciation and Thankfulness

Gratitude is an essential aspect of manifestation practice. It is the act of appreciating and expressing thankfulness for the blessings and abundance in our lives. Gratitude helps us to shift our focus from what we lack to what we have, creating a positive mindset that attracts more abundance and positivity into our lives. In this chapter, we will explore the power of gratitude and how it can help us to manifest our desires. We will provide real-life examples of how gratitude has transformed the lives of individuals, encouraging readers to incorporate gratitude into their daily lives.

The Science of Gratitude

The science of gratitude explores the psychological and neurological mechanisms behind gratitude and how it can have a profound impact on our well-being. When we experience gratitude, our brains release feel-good chemicals such as dopamine and serotonin, which are associated with positive emotions and increased happiness. Studies have shown that practicing gratitude can also improve sleep quality, decrease stress levels, and even strengthen the immune system. For example, a study conducted by the University of California found that people who practiced gratitude regularly had increased activity in the prefrontal cortex, the part of the brain responsible for regulating emotions and decision-making.

Benefits of Gratitude

Gratitude is a powerful tool that has numerous benefits on our mental, emotional, and physical health. Studies have shown that practicing gratitude can improve mood, increase feelings of happiness and contentment, reduce stress and anxiety, and even boost the immune system.

In addition to its effects on individual well-being, gratitude can also have a positive impact on our relationships, career, and overall life satisfaction. By expressing gratitude towards others, we can strengthen our relationships and build deeper connections. In the workplace, gratitude can increase employee motivation and productivity, as well as improve team morale and cohesion. And by focusing on what we are grateful for in our lives, we can cultivate a greater sense of fulfillment and purpose.

For example, imagine feeling grateful for your job and expressing that gratitude to your boss and colleagues. This can lead to increased job satisfaction, better relationships with coworkers, and potentially even career advancement opportunities. Similarly, expressing gratitude towards a partner can strengthen the bond between you and improve the overall quality of your relationship. By regularly practicing gratitude, we can experience these positive effects in all areas of our lives.

Techniques for Cultivating Gratitude

Gratitude is a powerful tool that can be cultivated through various techniques. In this section, we will discuss some strategies that can help you incorporate gratitude into your daily routines and habits.

One of the most effective ways to cultivate gratitude is through gratitude journaling. This involves writing down things you are grateful for on a regular basis, such as at the beginning or end of each day. For example, you could write about the people in your life who bring you joy, the things you have accomplished, or the opportunities you have been given.

Another technique for practicing gratitude is through gratitude meditations. This involves focusing your attention on things you are thankful for, and allowing yourself to experience the emotions associated with gratitude. You can do this by sitting in a quiet place and reflecting on the positive aspects of your life, or by listening to guided meditations that focus on gratitude.

Incorporating gratitude into your daily habits can also be done through small gestures, such as saying thank you to others or expressing appreciation for their efforts. This can help foster stronger relationships and create a more positive environment.

By incorporating these techniques into your daily life, you can begin to experience the many benefits of gratitude and enhance your overall sense of well-being.

Gratitude and Manifestation

Gratitude is a powerful tool in the manifestation process, as it helps us to focus on the abundance and positivity that already exist in our lives. When we express gratitude, we attract more of what we are thankful for, creating a positive cycle of manifestation. By focusing on what we have rather than what we lack, we open ourselves up to receiving more of what we desire.

For example, if you are trying to manifest financial abundance, expressing gratitude for the money you currently have can help to attract more money into your life. By focusing on the positive aspects of your financial situation, you are sending out a signal to the universe that you are open and receptive to receiving more abundance.

Similarly, if you are trying to manifest a loving relationship, expressing gratitude for the love and support you already have in your life can help to attract more love and positive relationships into your life. By focusing on the positive aspects of your current relationships, you are sending out a signal to the universe that you are open and receptive to receiving more love and positive connections.

In short, gratitude is an essential component of the manifestation process, as it helps us to focus on the positive aspects of our lives and attract more abundance and positivity into our experience.

Overcoming Challenges with Gratitude

When life gets tough, it can be challenging to find things to be grateful for. However, it's in these moments of hardship that practicing gratitude can be the most powerful. Here are some common obstacles to practicing gratitude and ways to overcome them:

- Negative thinking: Sometimes, our negative thoughts can overshadow any potential for gratitude. One way to combat negative thinking is to practice mindfulness and observe your thoughts without judgment. When you notice negative thoughts creeping in, try to shift your focus to something positive in your life.
- Difficult life circumstances: It can be hard to find gratitude when going through a tough time such as the loss of a loved one, illness, or financial struggles. In these situations, it can be helpful to focus on the small things that bring joy, such as a warm cup of tea or a good book. Also, reframing negative situations into a learning experience can help shift your perspective and find gratitude in the lessons learned.
- Lack of time: Some people feel they don't have time to practice gratitude, but it doesn't have to take a lot of time. You can take a few moments each day to reflect on

what you're thankful for or even incorporate gratitude into your daily routine, such as saying thank you for the food you eat.

Remember, gratitude is a mindset that can be developed with practice. By focusing on the good things in your life, even in challenging times, you can cultivate a sense of appreciation and attract more positivity into your life.

Gratitude is a powerful tool in manifestation. This chapter explores the science behind gratitude, its benefits, and techniques for cultivating it. By practicing gratitude, we can improve our well-being and attract positivity. Despite challenges, we can shift our perspective and find gratitude. Incorporating gratitude into our daily lives can lead to a more fulfilling and abundant existence.

CHAPTER VII

Taking Inspired Action: Aligning Yourself with Your Desires and Manifesting Your Goals

Welcome to the chapter on Taking Inspired Action. In this chapter, we will explore the crucial role of taking action in the manifestation process. Manifestation is not just about setting intentions and waiting for them to come true; it also requires taking inspired action towards our goals. We'll dive into how aligning ourselves with our desires and taking action can lead to manifestation success. Let's get started!

Aligned Action

Aligned action is the type of action that is taken in alignment with your true desires and goals. It differs from regular action in that it is intentional and purposeful, rather than simply going through the motions. Taking aligned action means that you are moving towards your goals with clarity and focus, rather than just taking random actions that may or may not get you there.

To identify aligned action, you must first be clear on what you truly desire. This requires introspection and self-reflection. Once you have clarity on your desires, you can start taking actions that are in alignment with them. For example, if your goal is to start a business, you might take aligned action by researching your market, developing a business plan, and networking with other entrepreneurs.

By taking aligned action towards your goals, you are sending a clear message to the universe about what you want to manifest. You are also creating momentum and energy towards your desires, making it more likely that they will come to fruition.

Overcoming Resistance

In order to manifest our desires, it's important to take inspired action. However, there can be many obstacles that prevent us from taking action, such as fear and limiting beliefs. In this chapter, we'll discuss common obstacles to taking action and strategies for overcoming resistance.

One of the most common obstacles to taking action is fear. We may be afraid of failure, or we may feel like we're not good enough to achieve our goals. Another obstacle is limiting beliefs, such as the belief that we don't have enough time or resources to accomplish what we want.

To overcome these obstacles, we can start by identifying our fears and limiting beliefs. Once we're aware of them, we can work to reframe our thinking and develop a more positive mindset. We can also break down our goals into smaller, more manageable steps, which can make them feel less daunting.

Another strategy for overcoming resistance is to enlist the help of others. We can seek out a coach or mentor who can provide guidance and support, or we can surround ourselves with like-minded individuals who can offer encouragement and motivation.

By overcoming resistance and taking inspired action towards our goals, we can move closer towards manifesting our desires and creating the life we truly want.

Visualization and Manifestation

Visualization is a powerful tool in taking inspired action towards manifesting your goals. By visualizing yourself already having achieved your desires, you can align yourself with that reality and take action from that place.

To use visualization in manifestation practice, start by setting a clear intention for what you want to manifest. Then, create a mental image or vision of yourself already having achieved that goal. Visualize the details of that reality, including how you feel, what you see, and who is around you.

As you visualize, allow yourself to fully immerse in the experience, using all your senses to create a vivid and compelling picture of your desired outcome. By doing this, you can tap into the positive emotions associated with achieving your goal, which can motivate you to take inspired action towards making it a reality.

Visualization can also help you identify the specific actions you need to take to manifest your desires. As you visualize, pay attention to any intuitive guidance or ideas that come to mind. These may be signs of the inspired action you need to take to align yourself with your desires and bring them into your reality.

For example, if your goal is to start your own business, you might visualize yourself running a successful company and feel the excitement and satisfaction that comes with it. As you visualize, you may receive the inspired action to start networking with other entrepreneurs or begin developing a business plan. By taking these actions, you can align yourself with the reality of being a successful business owner and manifest your desired outcome.

Tracking Progress

Tracking progress is an important aspect of taking inspired action towards manifesting your goals. By monitoring your progress, you can identify what's working well and what needs to be adjusted in your approach. This helps you stay on track and make necessary changes to achieve your desired outcome.

There are various methods for tracking progress, including creating a vision board, keeping a journal, or using a habit tracker app. For example, a vision board can help you visualize your goals and keep them top of mind, while a journal can help you reflect on your progress and identify any challenges or obstacles you may be facing.

Additionally, it's important to regularly check in with yourself and reassess your approach. If something isn't working, don't be afraid to make changes or try a new approach. The key is to stay flexible and open to adjustments as needed to stay on track towards your desired outcome.

By consistently tracking your progress and making adjustments as needed, you can maintain momentum towards manifesting your goals and ultimately achieve the success you desire.

In conclusion, taking inspired action is a crucial step in the manifestation process. By identifying and taking aligned action towards our goals, we can bring our desires into reality. However, there may be obstacles along the way, such as fear and limiting beliefs. It's important to overcome resistance and use visualization techniques to stay on track.

Tracking progress and making adjustments as needed is also essential in the manifestation process. By staying focused and taking consistent action, we can achieve our goals and live the life we desire.

I encourage you to take inspired action towards manifesting your goals. Remember, small steps can lead to big changes. Trust in the process and have faith that you can achieve what you desire.

CHAPTER VIII

Letting Go of Resistance: Overcoming Blocks and Limiting Beliefs

In this chapter, we will explore the concept of resistance and its impact on manifestation practice. Resistance refers to the obstacles and limiting beliefs that can hinder our ability to manifest our desires. We will discuss common forms of resistance and their underlying causes, as well as techniques for overcoming them. By letting go of resistance and cultivating a positive mindset, we can align ourselves with our desires and manifest the life we truly want.

Understanding Resistance

Types of resistance can be broadly categorized into internal and external types. Internal resistance can take the form of fear, self-doubt, limiting beliefs, and negative self-talk. External resistance can manifest as obstacles, setbacks, or challenges that seem to impede progress towards a desired outcome.

Fear is a common internal form of resistance that can keep individuals from taking action towards their goals. Fear of failure, fear of success, and fear of the unknown are examples of how fear can hinder manifestation practice. Limiting beliefs, which are often subconscious, can also act as a form of internal resistance. These beliefs can stem from past experiences, cultural or societal conditioning, or negative self-talk.

External resistance can take the form of challenges, obstacles, or setbacks that can derail progress towards manifestation. These challenges may come from outside sources, such as difficult circumstances or people, or they may arise from internal factors, such as lack of skills or resources.

To overcome resistance, it is important to identify the type of resistance and its source. By doing so, individuals can take steps to address the underlying issues and beliefs that may be hindering their progress towards their desired outcome.

Understanding Resistance

Resistance is a common obstacle in the manifestation practice that can hinder progress towards desired outcomes. Resistance can be categorized into internal and external types. Internal resistance can take the form of fear, self-doubt, limiting beliefs, and negative self-talk. External resistance can manifest as obstacles, setbacks, or challenges that seem to impede progress.

Fear and limiting beliefs can be particularly challenging forms of resistance that prevent individuals from taking action towards their goals. This type of resistance can create energetic blockages that clash with the positive energy needed for manifestation. It can also cause us to lose faith in the manifestation process, making it difficult to maintain a positive mindset and take inspired action.

To overcome resistance, it is important to identify the type of resistance and its source. By doing so, individuals can take steps to address the underlying issues and beliefs that may be hindering their progress towards their desired outcome. This involves acknowledging our fears and limiting beliefs, examining their origins, and consciously choosing to let go of them. By doing so, we can clear the energetic blockages and create a positive, aligned energy that supports the manifestation of our desires.

Identifying Limiting Beliefs

Identifying limiting beliefs is an essential step in overcoming resistance and manifesting our desired outcomes. Limiting beliefs are often deeply ingrained in our subconscious minds and can hold us back from reaching our full potential.

To identify limiting beliefs, we need to pay attention to our thoughts and feelings. When we find ourselves thinking negative thoughts or experiencing negative emotions, we can start to question the underlying beliefs that are driving them.

For example, if we find ourselves thinking "I'm not good enough" or "I don't deserve success," these thoughts may be rooted in limiting beliefs about our self-worth. By examining these beliefs, we can begin to challenge and reframe them in a more positive light.

Common limiting beliefs include beliefs about money, success, and relationships. For example, some people may believe that money is scarce and difficult to come by, or that they are not capable of achieving their desired level of success. These beliefs can create a scarcity mindset and prevent us from taking the necessary actions to manifest our desires.

Similarly, limiting beliefs about relationships can cause us to settle for less than we deserve or prevent us from pursuing fulfilling connections with others. For example, if we believe that we are unlovable or that we are not worthy of a healthy relationship, we may unconsciously sabotage our chances of finding love.

To address limiting beliefs, we need to first become aware of them and then consciously choose to replace them with more positive, empowering beliefs. This may involve working with a coach or therapist, practicing affirmations, or simply challenging negative thoughts as they arise.

Overcoming Limiting Beliefs

Overcoming limiting beliefs can be a challenging but essential aspect of manifesting your desires. Techniques such as reframing and visualization can be effective in addressing these beliefs and creating a positive mindset.

Reframing involves taking a negative belief and finding a new, positive way to view it. For example, instead of believing that "I am not good enough," you can reframe it as "I am constantly growing and improving." This helps to shift your mindset from a negative, limiting belief to a positive, empowering one.

Visualization can also be a powerful tool in overcoming limiting beliefs. By visualizing yourself achieving your desired outcome, you can create a positive, empowering image in your mind that can help to counteract any negative beliefs or self-doubt.

However, it is important to remember that simply reframing or visualizing is not enough to overcome limiting beliefs. Action is also crucial in overcoming these beliefs. Taking action towards your goals, even if it is small steps, can help to build confidence and reinforce positive beliefs.

For example, if you have a limiting belief that you are not good enough to start your own business, taking small steps such as researching or creating a business plan can help to build your confidence and show yourself that you are capable of achieving your goal.

Ultimately, the key to overcoming limiting beliefs is to take action and challenge yourself to push past your comfort zone. By doing so, you can create a positive, empowering mindset that supports your manifestation practice.

Letting Go of Fear

Fear can prevent us from manifesting our goals and reaching our full potential. It can keep us stuck in our comfort zone and prevent us from taking risks or pursuing our passions. However, there are strategies for overcoming fear and taking action towards our goals.

here are some techniques for overcoming fear:

- Identify the source of your fear and write it down.
- Challenge your fear by asking yourself if it's rational and realistic.
- Reframe your fear by focusing on the positive outcome you want to achieve.
- Practice visualization to imagine yourself overcoming your fear and achieving your goals.
- Take small steps towards your goals to gradually build confidence and reduce fear.
- Use positive affirmations to replace negative self-talk with supportive statements.
- Seek support from a therapist or coach to work through deep-seated fears and beliefs.
- Use relaxation techniques such as deep breathing or meditation to calm anxiety and fear.
- Create a plan of action and stick to it, even if you feel fear or resistance.
- Celebrate your successes and use them as motivation to continue taking action towards your goals.

Cultivating a Positive Mindset

A positive mindset plays a crucial role in the manifestation process as it aligns our energy with our desires, making it easier to attract them. Here are some techniques for cultivating a positive mindset:

- Affirmations: These are positive statements that are repeated to oneself to reinforce positive beliefs and change negative thought patterns. Examples of affirmations include "I am worthy of abundance," "I am capable of achieving my goals," and "I trust the universe to bring me what I desire."
- Gratitude: Focusing on gratitude helps to shift our perspective from what we lack to what we already have, creating a sense of abundance and positivity. A gratitude practice can involve keeping a daily gratitude journal or simply taking a few minutes each day to reflect on things we are grateful for.
- Visualization: Visualization involves mentally visualizing oneself in the desired outcome, feeling the emotions associated with it, and imagining it as already achieved. This technique helps to create a positive energy and belief in the manifestation of the desired outcome.
- Self-care: Taking care of oneself through practices such as exercise, healthy eating, and meditation can help to reduce stress and cultivate a positive mindset.
- Surrounding oneself with positivity: Spending time with positive and supportive people, consuming uplifting media, and engaging in activities that bring joy can also help to cultivate a positive mindset.

By incorporating these techniques into one's daily practice, individuals can cultivate a positive mindset that supports the manifestation of their desires.

Surrendering to the Universe

The manifestation process involves setting intentions and taking inspired action towards achieving our desires. However, sometimes we can become too focused on controlling every aspect of the process, which can create resistance and block the flow of positive energy needed for manifestation. This is where the concept of surrendering and letting go comes in.

Surrendering in manifestation practice means releasing our attachment to specific outcomes and trusting the universe to deliver what is best for us. It involves relinquishing the need to control every detail and instead, allowing things to unfold naturally. Surrendering is not about giving up on our goals or taking a passive approach, but rather, it's about surrendering the outcome to the universe while remaining actively engaged in the process.

There are several benefits to surrendering and releasing control in manifestation practice:

Reducing Resistance: When we try to control every aspect of the manifestation process, we can create resistance, which blocks the flow of positive energy. Surrendering helps us to release this resistance and allow positive energy to flow more freely.

Letting Go of Limiting Beliefs: When we surrender, we let go of our limiting beliefs and trust that the universe has our best interests at heart. This can help to shift our mindset and open us up to new possibilities and opportunities.

Finding Peace and Acceptance: Surrendering can bring a sense of peace and acceptance, knowing that we have done everything we can to manifest our desires, and now it's up to the universe to take care of the rest.

Allowing for Serendipity: When we release control, we allow for serendipitous events and unexpected opportunities to present themselves, which can lead to even greater manifestations than we originally envisioned.

In conclusion, letting go and surrendering to the universe is a crucial aspect of manifestation practice. By releasing resistance and limiting beliefs, we open ourselves up to the abundance of the universe and allow our desires to manifest more easily. It takes courage and effort to let go of control, but the benefits are well worth it. Keep practicing and trusting in the universe, and watch as your dreams become reality.

CHAPTER IX

Understanding the Role of Emotions: How Your Feelings Affect Manifestation

Emotions are complex psychological and physiological responses to stimuli that can be experienced as positive or negative. They are a fundamental part of the human experience and play a significant role in shaping our thoughts, behaviors, and overall well-being. Emotions can arise from a variety of sources, such as external events, internal thoughts and beliefs, and physical sensations.

Emotions are closely tied to manifestation practice, as they can significantly impact our ability to attract the things we desire. When we feel positive emotions such as joy, love, and gratitude, we are more likely to be in a state of alignment with our desires, which can increase the likelihood of manifestation. Conversely, negative emotions such as fear, doubt, and anxiety can create resistance and blockages that make it more difficult to manifest what we want.

How Emotions Affect Manifestation ?

Emotions play a crucial role in the manifestation process. The Law of Attraction states that like attracts like, meaning that the energy we emit attracts similar energy back to us. This energy is determined by our emotional vibration. When we feel good, we emit a high vibration, and when we feel bad, we emit a low vibration.

Negative emotions such as fear, doubt, and anxiety can lower our emotional vibration and attract negative experiences into our lives. For example, if we constantly worry about not having enough money, we may continue to experience financial struggles because we are emitting a low vibration of lack and scarcity.

On the other hand, positive emotions such as joy, gratitude, and love can raise our emotional vibration and attract positive experiences into our lives. When we feel grateful for what we have, we emit a high vibration of abundance, and we attract more abundance into our lives.

For instance, if we are looking to manifest a loving relationship, we need to emit a high vibration of love and happiness to attract a partner who is also emitting a similar vibration. This means that we need to focus on feeling good and radiating positive emotions to the universe to manifest our desires.

Techniques for Managing Emotions

A. Mindfulness and emotional awareness:

- Mindfulness is the practice of being present and fully engaged in the present moment, without judgment.
- By cultivating mindfulness, we can become more aware of our emotions and the impact they have on our thoughts and actions.
- This can help us identify negative emotions and work towards managing them.

B. Techniques for managing negative emotions:

- There are several techniques for managing negative emotions, such as deep breathing, meditation, and journaling.
- Deep breathing can help calm the nervous system and reduce stress.

- Meditation can help us become more centered and grounded, and can also increase positive emotions such as compassion and gratitude.
- Journaling can help us identify patterns in our emotions and thoughts, and can also provide an outlet for expressing and processing our emotions.

C. Cultivating positive emotions through gratitude and visualization:

- Gratitude is the practice of focusing on the things we are thankful for in our lives, and can help shift our perspective to a more positive one.
- Visualization is the practice of imagining positive outcomes and experiences, which can help increase positive emotions and reduce negative ones.
- By regularly practicing gratitude and visualization, we can cultivate a more positive emotional state, which can in turn enhance our manifestation practice.

Overcoming Emotional Blocks

Emotional blocks are often caused by past experiences, limiting beliefs, and negative self-talk, which can hinder our ability to manifest our desires. Here are some techniques for overcoming emotional blocks:

A. Identifying and addressing emotional blocks to manifestation:

- Journaling: Writing down our thoughts and feelings can help us identify negative patterns and emotional blocks.
- Self-reflection: Taking time to reflect on our emotions and past experiences can help us identify and address emotional blocks.

- Therapy: Talking to a therapist can help us identify and work through emotional blocks.

B. Techniques for releasing negative emotions:

- Meditation: Practicing meditation can help us release negative emotions and reduce stress and anxiety.
- Breathwork: Focused breathing techniques can help us release negative emotions and promote relaxation.
- EFT Tapping: Emotional Freedom Technique (EFT) Tapping is a technique that involves tapping on specific points on the body while focusing on negative emotions, which can help release them.

C. The role of self-care in managing emotions:

- Self-care practices like exercise, getting enough sleep, and eating a healthy diet can help us manage our emotions.
- Setting boundaries and saying no to things that don't serve us can help us manage our emotional energy.
- Practicing self-compassion and self-love can help us develop a positive emotional state and overcome emotional blocks.

By identifying and addressing emotional blocks, releasing negative emotions, and practicing self-care, we can overcome emotional barriers to manifestation and create a positive emotional state that supports our goals and desires

In conclusion, understanding the role of emotions is crucial in manifestation practice. Our emotions have a significant impact on the law of attraction and can either support or hinder our manifestations. By practicing emotional awareness, managing negative emotions, and cultivating positive ones, we can overcome emotional blocks and achieve our desired outcomes. Remember, you have the power to control your emotions and manifest the life you desire.

CHAPTER X

Manifesting Abundance: Attracting Wealth and Prosperity

Abundance can be defined as having more than enough of what we need, whether it be wealth, love, health, or any other aspect of our lives. It is the feeling of being fulfilled, satisfied, and prosperous in all areas of our lives.

Abundance is a key component of manifestation practice, as the law of attraction is based on the principle of like attracts like. When we focus on abundance, we attract more abundance into our lives. By aligning our thoughts, beliefs, and actions with abundance, we can manifest the life we desire.

Cultivating abundance in our lives is important for our personal growth and fulfillment. When we have an abundance mindset, we are more likely to take risks, pursue our passions, and live a life of purpose. Abundance allows us to live in a state of joy and gratitude, rather than scarcity and lack.

Understanding the Law of Attraction and Abundance

When it comes to manifesting abundance, the Law of Attraction plays a crucial role. This law states that we attract into our lives whatever we focus on and put our energy towards. In other words, our thoughts and beliefs can shape our reality. By adopting a positive and abundance-focused mindset, we can manifest wealth and prosperity into our lives.

Belief and mindset are key components in attracting abundance. By having a strong belief in our ability to create wealth and abundance, we can overcome any limiting beliefs that might be holding us back. Our mindset also plays a critical role in attracting abundance, as a positive outlook can help us focus on opportunities and possibilities rather than limitations and obstacles.

Gratitude is another essential factor in attracting abundance. When we focus on what we are grateful for, we are more likely to attract more positive experiences and abundance into our lives. Gratitude helps shift our focus away from lack and scarcity towards abundance and opportunity.

Strategies for Attracting Wealth and Prosperity

- Setting clear intentions and goals for abundance: It's important to have a clear vision of what abundance means to you and set specific goals related to wealth and prosperity. This helps to focus your energy and attention towards achieving your desired outcome.
- Identifying and overcoming limiting beliefs around money: Many people hold limiting beliefs around money that can prevent them from manifesting abundance. It's important to identify and release these beliefs, such as "money is the root of all evil" or "I don't deserve to be wealthy", in order to open up to the flow of abundance.
- Taking inspired action towards abundance: Manifestation is not just about positive thinking; it also involves taking inspired action towards your goals. This means following your intuition and taking steps towards your desired outcome, even if they may seem scary or outside of your comfort zone.
- Using visualization techniques to manifest abundance: Visualization is a powerful manifestation technique that

involves imagining yourself already in possession of the abundance you desire. This can help to create a positive emotional state and attract more abundance into your life.

Using these strategies together can help to create a powerful manifestation practice for attracting wealth and prosperity. It's important to stay committed to your goals and keep a positive mindset, even when faced with challenges or setbacks.

Cultivating an Abundance Mindset

The role of mindset in attracting wealth and prosperity: Having a positive and abundant mindset can play a significant role in attracting wealth and prosperity. A person's mindset determines how they perceive and respond to opportunities and challenges in life. It can either limit or expand their potential for success.

Techniques for cultivating an abundance mindset, such as affirmations and gratitude: To cultivate an abundance mindset, one must focus on positive thinking, affirmations, and gratitude. Affirmations are positive statements that help to reprogram the mind and shift it towards positive thinking. Gratitude practice involves focusing on the blessings and abundance already present in one's life, which creates more positive energy and attracts more abundance.

The benefits of adopting an abundance mindset in all areas of life: When an individual adopts an abundance mindset, they begin to see more opportunities for growth and success in all areas of life, not just financial. They become more open to new experiences and take more risks, leading to personal growth and fulfillment. It also helps to reduce stress and anxiety and improves overall well-being.

Overcoming Blocks to Abundance

When it comes to manifesting abundance, it's not uncommon to experience blocks that prevent us from achieving our goals. These blocks can take many forms, such as limiting beliefs around money, negative emotions, and self-sabotaging behaviors.

To overcome these blocks, it's important to first identify them and understand where they're coming from. Are they based on past experiences or societal conditioning? Once we've pinpointed the source of our limiting beliefs, we can start to work on releasing them.

One effective strategy for releasing limiting beliefs is to practice positive affirmations. By repeatedly affirming positive statements about ourselves and our financial situation, we can reprogram our subconscious mind to support our goals. Another strategy is to practice visualization techniques, which can help us to create a clear mental picture of what we want to manifest.

It's also important to address any negative emotions we may have around money. For example, we may feel guilty or ashamed about wanting to manifest wealth and prosperity. By acknowledging and releasing these negative emotions, we can create a more positive relationship with abundance.

Finally, self-care plays a crucial role in cultivating a positive relationship with abundance. This means taking care of our physical, emotional, and mental well-being, and treating ourselves with kindness and compassion. When we feel good about ourselves and our lives, we're better able to attract the abundance we desire.

In conclusion, manifesting abundance and attracting wealth and prosperity is possible through understanding and utilizing the Law of Attraction, setting clear intentions, cultivating an abundance mindset, and overcoming blocks to abundance. By adopting these strategies and incorporating self-care practices, individuals can open themselves up to greater opportunities for abundance and fulfillment in all areas of life.

CHAPTER XI

Manifesting Relationships: Finding and Attracting the Right Partner

In this chapter, we will explore the concept of manifesting relationships and how it can help you find and attract the right partner. We'll begin by defining what a fulfilling relationship looks like and why it's essential to manifest the right partner. We'll also discuss the common misconceptions about manifesting relationships and how to approach this process with the right mindset.

Having a fulfilling relationship is one of the most crucial aspects of leading a happy and satisfying life. However, finding the right partner can be challenging, and many people struggle to manifest a relationship that aligns with their values, beliefs, and goals. This is where the concept of manifesting relationships comes into play. By harnessing the power of the Law of Attraction, you can attract a partner who is a perfect match for you in every way.

Understanding the Law of Attraction in Relationships

The Law of Attraction applies not only to material possessions and career success, but also to relationships. It is based on the principle that like attracts like, meaning that the thoughts and emotions you project out into the world will attract similar thoughts and emotions back to you. In the context of relationships, this means that if you consistently focus on negative thoughts and emotions, you are likely to attract negative relationships or experiences. On the other hand, if you focus on positive thoughts and emotions, you are more likely to attract positive relationships and experiences.

For instance, if you constantly think about how difficult it is to find a partner, or how all relationships end in heartbreak, you are unconsciously sending out negative energy into the universe, which may hinder your ability to attract a fulfilling relationship. However, if you focus on positive affirmations such as "I am deserving of a loving and fulfilling relationship" or "I am attracting my ideal partner," you are more likely to attract positive relationship experiences.

Moreover, the Law of Attraction is not only about attracting a partner, but also about attracting a relationship that aligns with your desires and values. This is why it is crucial to clarify your relationship goals and desires. By doing so, you are setting a clear intention and giving the universe a roadmap to follow in manifesting the relationship that is right for you.

Clarifying Your Relationship Goals and Desires

Clarifying your relationship goals and desires is a crucial step in manifesting the right partner. Before you can attract the ideal partner, you must first have a clear idea of what you want in a relationship. This involves taking the time to reflect on your values, interests, and personal goals. Consider the qualities you seek in a partner, such as their personality traits, lifestyle, and communication style. It's important to also identify any deal-breakers or non-negotiables you have.

Once you have a clear understanding of what you want in a relationship, you can start to use the power of visualization and affirmations to attract the right partner. Visualization involves picturing yourself in a happy and fulfilling relationship, while affirmations are positive statements that you repeat to yourself to shift your mindset towards attracting the right partner. For example, you might repeat affirmations such as "I am worthy of a loving and healthy relationship" or "I am attracting the right partner into my life".

By clarifying your relationship goals and desires and using visualization and affirmations, you can start to shift your focus towards attracting the right partner and create a positive energy around your search for love.

Overcoming Limiting Beliefs and Blocks to Love

Limiting beliefs and emotional blocks can be major obstacles to manifesting a fulfilling relationship. Some common limiting beliefs include thinking that love is scarce, believing that one is not worthy of love, or holding onto past hurts and resentments. These beliefs can create a negative energy that repels potential partners and keeps us stuck in unfulfilling relationships.

To overcome these blocks, it's important to identify and release them. This can involve practices such as journaling, therapy, or energy work to uncover and release negative emotions and beliefs. Affirmations and visualization techniques can also be powerful tools for reprogramming the mind to attract positive relationships.

In addition, cultivating self-love and self-care is essential in attracting a healthy relationship. When we love and value ourselves, we are more likely to attract partners who share those qualities and treat us with respect and kindness. This can involve practices such as setting boundaries, taking care of our physical and emotional well-being, and nurturing our passions and interests.

Overall, releasing limiting beliefs and cultivating self-love and care are crucial steps in attracting and manifesting a healthy, fulfilling relationship.

Taking Inspired Action Towards Finding Love

Once you have clarified your relationship goals and desires, it's important to take inspired action towards manifesting the right partner. This means taking action that is aligned with your desired relationship and that feels good to you. For example, if you want to meet someone who shares your interests, you might join a club or group that revolves around those interests. Or, if you're looking for a serious relationship, you might try online dating or attend social events with a mindset of being open to meeting new people.

However, it's important to remember that taking action doesn't mean forcing or pushing for a relationship. It's about being open and receptive to opportunities that align with your desires. This can mean being willing to step out of your comfort zone, try new things, and connect with new people.

Being open and receptive also means letting go of any attachment to a specific outcome. Trust that the Universe has your best interest in mind and that the right partner will come into your life at the right time. By taking inspired action and staying open to opportunities, you'll be on your way to manifesting a fulfilling relationship.

In conclusion, manifesting the right partner requires clarity, self-reflection, and a positive mindset. By understanding the Law of Attraction, clarifying your relationship goals and desires, overcoming limiting beliefs and blocks to love, and taking inspired action, you can attract a fulfilling and healthy relationship. Remember that attracting the right partner is not just about finding someone else, but also about cultivating a loving relationship with yourself. Through self-love and self-care, you can create a positive energy that attracts the right person into your life. Trust the universe and believe that you deserve to find the love you desire. With these principles and strategies, you can manifest the relationship of your dreams.

CHAPTER XII

Manifesting Health and Wellness: Achieving Vibrant Physical and Emotional Well-being

In this chapter, we will explore the concept of manifesting health and wellness. Health and wellness can be defined as a state of complete physical, mental, and social well-being, and not merely the absence of disease or infirmity. It is a holistic approach to well-being that encompasses all aspects of a person's life.

The importance of manifesting vibrant physical and emotional well-being cannot be overstated. When we are healthy and well, we have the energy, clarity, and motivation to pursue our goals and dreams. We are more resilient in the face of challenges, and we experience greater joy and fulfillment in our daily lives. Therefore, it is essential to learn how to manifest health and wellness in our lives so that we can live our best lives and achieve our highest potential. In the following sections, we will explore various strategies and techniques for manifesting vibrant physical and emotional well-being.

Understanding the Mind-Body Connection

The mind and body are deeply interconnected, and our thoughts and emotions have a significant impact on our physical health. Research has shown that chronic stress, anxiety, and negative thought patterns can contribute to a range of health problems, including heart disease, depression, and autoimmune disorders. On the other hand, cultivating a positive mindset can help improve overall well-being and resilience.

Techniques such as mindfulness meditation, deep breathing exercises, and visualization can help cultivate a healthy mind-body connection by reducing stress and promoting relaxation. Practicing gratitude and positive self-talk can also help shift negative thought patterns and promote a more positive outlook.

It's important to recognize that achieving vibrant physical and emotional well-being requires a holistic approach that addresses both the mind and body. By cultivating a healthy mind-body connection, we can support our overall health and well-being, and increase our capacity for joy and fulfillment in life

Setting Health and Wellness Goals

Setting clear goals for health and wellness is an important step in manifesting vibrant physical and emotional well-being. By setting specific and achievable goals, individuals can clarify their priorities and take action towards improving their overall health.

To begin, it's important to identify what areas of your health you want to focus on. This could include physical health goals such as losing weight, improving cardiovascular health, or increasing strength and flexibility. It could also include emotional health goals such as reducing stress, improving self-esteem, or enhancing relationships.

Once you have identified your goals, it's important to prioritize them and create a plan for achieving them. This could involve breaking down larger goals into smaller, more manageable steps, and setting deadlines for each step along the way. It's also important to track your progress and adjust your plan as necessary.

Visualization and affirmation can be powerful tools in achieving health and wellness goals. By visualizing yourself as healthy, vibrant, and energetic, and repeating affirmations such as "I am healthy and strong," you can program your mind to focus on positive outcomes and help manifest your desired state of well-being.

Cultivating Healthy Habits

Cultivating healthy habits is crucial in achieving vibrant physical and emotional well-being. Here are some techniques and strategies for developing and maintaining healthy habits:

- Start small: Begin with simple, achievable changes such as drinking more water, taking a 10-minute walk, or eating more fruits and vegetables.
- Make it enjoyable: Choose healthy activities that you enjoy, such as dancing, hiking, or playing a sport. This can help you stay motivated and committed to your healthy habits.
- Create a routine: Incorporate healthy habits into your daily routine, such as meditating in the morning, going for a walk after dinner, or practicing yoga before bed.
- Get support: Seek support from friends, family, or a healthcare professional to help you stay on track and hold you accountable.
- Overcome obstacles: Identify common obstacles to healthy living, such as lack of time, stress, or temptation, and develop strategies to overcome them. For example, you could schedule your workouts in advance, practice stress-reducing techniques, or keep healthy snacks on hand.
- By cultivating healthy habits, you can improve your physical and emotional well-being and live a more

fulfilling life.

Nurturing emotional wellness

Nurturing emotional wellness is essential for achieving vibrant physical and emotional well-being. Stress, anxiety, and negative emotions can take a toll on the body and lead to various health problems. Here are some strategies for managing stress and anxiety and cultivating positive emotions and mindset:

- Practice mindfulness: Mindfulness is a technique that involves being fully present and engaged in the current moment. Mindfulness can help reduce stress and anxiety and improve emotional well-being.
- Engage in physical activity: Exercise releases endorphins, which are natural mood boosters. Regular physical activity can help reduce stress and anxiety and improve emotional well-being.
- Connect with loved ones: Spending time with friends and family and engaging in social activities can help improve emotional wellness and reduce feelings of loneliness and isolation.
- Practice gratitude: Focusing on the good things in your life and expressing gratitude can help cultivate a positive mindset and improve emotional well-being.
- Seek support: If you're struggling with stress, anxiety, or other emotional challenges, don't hesitate to seek professional support. Talking to a therapist or counselor can help you develop coping strategies and improve emotional well-being.
- By incorporating these strategies into your daily routine, you can nurture your emotional wellness and achieve vibrant physical and emotional well-being.

In conclusion, manifesting health and wellness is an important aspect of a fulfilling and happy life. It involves understanding the mind-body connection, setting clear goals, cultivating healthy habits, and nurturing emotional well-being. By applying the principles of manifestation to health and wellness, individuals can achieve vibrant physical and emotional well-being. It requires taking intentional action and making a commitment to prioritizing self-care. With patience, persistence, and a positive mindset, anyone can manifest a healthy and fulfilling life.

CHAPTER XIII

Overcoming Obstacles: Turning Challenges into Opportunities for Growth

Understanding Obstacles and their Impact on Growth

When it comes to personal growth, obstacles and challenges are inevitable. They can come in many forms, including physical, emotional, financial, or professional. However, these obstacles don't have to be viewed as insurmountable roadblocks. Instead, they can be seen as opportunities for growth and transformation.

To help you understand obstacles and their impact on growth, consider the following points:

- Defining obstacles and challenges: An obstacle is anything that stands in the way of achieving a desired goal or outcome. It can be a physical, emotional, or mental barrier that prevents progress. Challenges are similar to obstacles, but they are typically viewed as more difficult or demanding situations.
- Identifying common obstacles and their impact on personal growth: Common obstacles can include fear, self-doubt, lack of confidence, limited resources, or past traumas. These obstacles can hinder personal growth and prevent individuals from reaching their full potential.
- Recognizing opportunities for growth and learning in overcoming obstacles: Overcoming obstacles can lead to personal growth and learning. By confronting and

overcoming obstacles, individuals can develop resilience, creativity, problem-solving skills, and a greater sense of self-awareness.

Overall, it's important to understand that obstacles and challenges are a natural part of the growth process. They can be difficult and frustrating, but they also provide opportunities for learning and personal transformation.

Strategies for Overcoming Obstacles

Strategies for overcoming obstacles involve developing specific skills and techniques that can help you navigate challenges effectively. Here are some ways to overcome obstacles:

1. Develop resilience and mental toughness: Resilience is the ability to adapt to difficult situations and bounce back from adversity. It involves developing a positive mindset, practicing self-care, and building a strong support network. Mental toughness is the ability to stay focused, motivated, and committed to your goals despite challenges or setbacks. It involves developing a growth mindset, setting realistic expectations, and maintaining a sense of purpose and meaning in life.
2. Practice problem-solving and decision-making: These skills involve identifying problems, evaluating possible solutions, and making informed decisions. To improve problem-solving and decision-making skills, try to break down problems into smaller parts, brainstorm creative solutions, and seek feedback from others. It's also important to weigh the pros and cons of different options and consider the potential consequences of your decisions.

3. Embrace creativity and innovation: Sometimes, overcoming obstacles requires thinking outside the box and coming up with new, innovative solutions. This involves exploring different perspectives, generating new ideas, and taking calculated risks. To cultivate creativity and innovation, try to expose yourself to new experiences and ideas, collaborate with others, and experiment with different approaches.

By developing these skills and techniques, you can overcome obstacles with greater ease and confidence, and ultimately achieve your goals. Remember that obstacles can be opportunities for growth and learning, so embrace the challenge and use it to your advantage.

Overcoming Fear and Self-Doubt

Overcoming fear and self-doubt is crucial in achieving personal growth and success. Fear and self-doubt can hold us back from pursuing our goals and dreams, and they can limit our potential. Understanding the root causes of fear and self-doubt is the first step in overcoming them. Often, fear and self-doubt stem from negative experiences in our past or limiting beliefs we hold about ourselves. To overcome fear and self-doubt, we need to identify these negative thought patterns and replace them with positive affirmations.

Building confidence and self-esteem is another key strategy for overcoming fear and self-doubt. We can do this by setting achievable goals and celebrating our successes along the way. It's also important to surround ourselves with positive and supportive people who can lift us up and encourage us to keep going.

Mindset shifts are another powerful tool for overcoming fear and self-doubt. We can learn to reframe our negative thoughts and beliefs and focus on positive outcomes instead. For example, instead of thinking, "I'm not good enough," we can shift our mindset to, "I am capable of learning and growing."

Coping with Change and Uncertainty

Change is an inevitable part of life, and it can often bring about feelings of uncertainty and discomfort. However, it is important to recognize that change can also present opportunities for growth and personal development. By learning how to cope with change and uncertainty, individuals can develop greater resilience and adaptability, which can be invaluable skills in both personal and professional settings.

One of the first steps in coping with change and uncertainty is to acknowledge and accept that it is a natural part of life. This can involve recognizing that change can bring about feelings of fear, anxiety, or even excitement, and that these feelings are normal and valid. From there, individuals can begin to develop strategies for adapting to change and uncertainty.

Some techniques for coping with change and uncertainty include:

1. Developing a growth mindset: This involves embracing the idea that challenges and setbacks are opportunities for growth and learning, rather than signs of failure or inadequacy. By adopting a growth mindset, individuals can approach change with a sense of curiosity and openness, rather than fear or resistance.
2. Seeking support: Change can be difficult to navigate alone, and it can be helpful to seek support from friends, family members, or mental health professionals. Talking about one's feelings and experiences can help to process

emotions and gain a new perspective on the situation.

3. Engaging in self-care: Prioritizing self-care, such as getting enough sleep, exercise, and healthy food, can help to build resilience and reduce stress levels. Engaging in activities that bring joy and fulfillment, such as hobbies or spending time in nature, can also help to cultivate a sense of well-being.
4. Practicing mindfulness: Mindfulness involves paying attention to the present moment, without judgment or distraction. By practicing mindfulness, individuals can develop greater self-awareness and learn to observe their thoughts and feelings without becoming overwhelmed by them. This can help to reduce stress and promote a sense of calm.
5. Setting goals: Setting goals can provide a sense of direction and purpose, even in the face of uncertainty. By setting achievable goals, individuals can build momentum and confidence, and develop a sense of control over their circumstances.

Turning Setbacks into Comebacks

Life is unpredictable, and setbacks are inevitable. However, it's not the setback that defines you but how you respond to it. When we experience failures or setbacks, it's natural to feel demotivated, disappointed, or even frustrated. But, with a growth mindset and the right strategies, we can reframe these setbacks into opportunities for growth and come back even stronger. Here are some tips for turning setbacks into comebacks:

- Reframe setbacks as opportunities for growth: Instead of dwelling on the negative aspects of the setback, try to focus on the lessons learned and how you can use this experience to improve yourself. Reframing the setback as an opportunity for growth can help you stay motivated and optimistic.

- Strategize for bouncing back: It's essential to have a plan in place for how you'll recover from a setback. Identify the specific steps you need to take to overcome the challenge and make progress towards your goals. Be prepared to adjust your plan as needed and to seek support from others when necessary.
- Embrace a growth mindset: A growth mindset is the belief that we can develop and improve our abilities through hard work and persistence. Embracing this mindset can help you stay motivated and focused on the long-term, even when faced with setbacks.
- Harness the power of perseverance: Perseverance is the ability to persist in the face of difficulty or adversity. It's a critical trait to have when bouncing back from setbacks. When you encounter obstacles or setbacks, try to stay committed to your goals and keep pushing forward.

Remember, setbacks are a natural part of life, and it's not the setback itself that defines you, but how you respond to it. By reframing setbacks as opportunities for growth, strategizing for bouncing back, embracing a growth mindset, and harnessing the power of perseverance, you can turn setbacks into comebacks and achieve even greater success.

CHAPTER XIV

Living the Law of Attraction: Integrating the Principles into Your Daily Life

Understanding the Law of Attraction

The Law of Attraction is a principle that states that like attracts like. This means that the energy you put out into the universe will attract similar energy back to you. The Law of Attraction is based on the belief that your thoughts and feelings have a powerful effect on your life and can attract positive or negative experiences.

The science behind the Law of Attraction is rooted in the principles of quantum physics. Quantum physics has shown that everything in the universe is made up of energy, including our thoughts and emotions. This energy vibrates at different frequencies, and similar frequencies are attracted to each other.

Despite its popularity, the Law of Attraction is often misunderstood and subject to myths and misconceptions. Some people believe that the Law of Attraction is simply wishful thinking, while others think that it is a magical solution that can instantly manifest anything they desire. However, the Law of Attraction is based on the principles of manifestation, which require effort, focus, and action in addition to positive thoughts and feelings.

Aligning Your Thoughts and Emotions with Your Desires

The Law of Attraction is a powerful tool that can be used to manifest our desires, but it all begins with our mindset.

Positive thinking is crucial in the manifestation process. When we focus our thoughts on what we want rather than what we don't want, we attract more positive experiences into our lives. Here are some ways to cultivate a positive mindset:

1. Identify and Release Limiting Beliefs: Limiting beliefs are negative thoughts that hold us back from achieving our goals. These beliefs often stem from past experiences or societal conditioning. To identify limiting beliefs, pay attention to the negative thoughts that come up when you think about your goals. Once you've identified them, reframe them into positive affirmations. For example, if your limiting belief is "I'm not good enough," reframe it as "I am capable of achieving my goals."
2. Cultivate Gratitude: Gratitude is a powerful tool that can shift our focus from what we lack to what we have. When we focus on what we're grateful for, we attract more abundance into our lives. A simple way to cultivate gratitude is to keep a gratitude journal. Write down three things you're grateful for every day, and focus on the positive aspects of your life.
3. Embrace an Abundance Mindset: An abundance mindset is the belief that there is enough of everything to go around. When we believe in abundance, we attract more abundance into our lives. To cultivate an abundance mindset, focus on what you have rather than what you lack. Visualize abundance in all areas of your life, and trust that the universe will provide.

Taking Inspired Action towards Your Goals

The Law of Attraction is not just about positive thinking and visualization, it also requires taking action towards your desires. Here are some strategies for manifesting your goals through action:

1. Setting inspired goals: Instead of just setting arbitrary goals, identify the ones that truly inspire and excite you. This will help you stay motivated and committed to taking action towards them.
2. Breaking down goals into manageable steps: Big goals can often feel overwhelming, but breaking them down into smaller, more manageable steps can make them feel more attainable. This also allows you to celebrate your progress along the way.
3. Taking consistent action: Consistent action is key to manifesting your desires. This means making a habit of taking small steps towards your goals every day, even when you don't feel motivated or inspired.
4. Being open and receptive to opportunities: Sometimes the universe will present you with unexpected opportunities that can help you achieve your goals. Being open and receptive to these opportunities can help you manifest your desires more quickly.
5. Adjusting your approach when necessary: Sometimes the actions you take towards your goals may not be effective. It's important to stay flexible and open-minded, and be willing to adjust your approach if necessary.

By taking action towards your goals and staying open to opportunities, you can manifest your desires and live a life that aligns with your deepest desires and values.

Maintaining a High Vibration for Manifestation

The Law of Attraction is based on the principle that everything in the universe is made up of energy, including our thoughts and emotions. When we focus our thoughts and emotions on positive things, we attract positive energy and experiences into our lives. Understanding the power of vibration in the Law of Attraction is essential to manifesting our desires.

Raising our vibration is a critical component of the Law of Attraction because our vibration determines the quality of the energy we attract into our lives. To raise our vibration, we must first become aware of our thoughts and emotions and focus on cultivating positive ones. Here are some techniques for raising your vibration:

- Gratitude: Cultivating gratitude is a powerful way to raise your vibration. By focusing on the things you are thankful for, you shift your energy from lack to abundance.
- Visualization: Visualization is another technique for raising your vibration. By visualizing yourself already having what you desire, you align your energy with that reality and attract it into your life.
- Affirmations: Affirmations are positive statements that you repeat to yourself. By affirming what you desire as already being true, you raise your vibration and attract it into your life.

Maintaining a high vibration in daily life is crucial for manifesting our desires. Here are some strategies for maintaining a high vibration:

- Self-care: Taking care of your physical and emotional well-being is critical to maintaining a high vibration.

Eating well, getting enough rest, exercising, and engaging in activities you enjoy can all help raise your vibration.

- Surround yourself with positivity: Surrounding yourself with positive people, places, and things can help you maintain a high vibration. Avoid negative news, gossip, and people who bring you down.
- Let go of resistance: Resistance to what is can lower your vibration. Learning to accept what is and let go of resistance can help you maintain a high vibration.

By understanding the power of vibration in the Law of Attraction, raising our vibration, and maintaining a high vibration, we can manifest our desires and live the life we desire

Integrating the Law of Attraction into Your Daily Life

Applying the Law of Attraction in everyday life requires a conscious effort and practice. Here are some practical tips for integrating this powerful law into your daily routines:

- Cultivate gratitude: One of the most effective ways to raise your vibration and attract more abundance into your life is by practicing gratitude. Start your day by expressing gratitude for the blessings in your life and make it a habit to appreciate the small things that bring you joy throughout the day. This simple practice will help you shift your focus from what you lack to what you have, and increase your vibration.
- Practice positive affirmations: Affirmations are powerful tools that can help you reprogram your mind and change your beliefs. Identify the areas of your life that you want to improve and create positive affirmations that support your desired outcome. Repeat

them daily, and as you do, visualize yourself already living your desired reality.

- Stay aligned with your desires: To manifest your desires, you need to stay aligned with them. This means that you need to focus on the feeling of already having what you want, rather than the lack of it. Keep your thoughts, emotions, and actions in alignment with your desires, and trust that the universe will bring you what you need at the right time.
- Take inspired action: While the Law of Attraction is a powerful tool, it requires action on your part. Take inspired action towards your goals, and trust that the universe will support you along the way. Stay open to opportunities and be willing to take risks and step out of your comfort zone.
- Practice self-care: Self-care is essential for maintaining a high vibration and staying aligned with your desires. Take care of your physical, mental, and emotional health, and make time for activities that bring you joy and relaxation. When you feel good, you attract more good things into your life.

By integrating these practical tips into your daily routines, you can cultivate a manifesting mindset and attract more abundance, joy, and fulfillment into your life. Remember, the Law of Attraction is a powerful tool, but it requires consistency, dedication, and a willingness to believe in the power of the universe to bring you what you desire.

CHAPTER XV

The Science behind the Law of Attraction: Understanding Quantum Physics and Attraction

The Basics of Quantum Physics: An Overview

Quantum physics is a branch of physics that studies the behavior of matter and energy at the subatomic level. It deals with the fundamental building blocks of the universe, including atoms, electrons, and photons. At this level, the classical laws of physics break down, and strange phenomena such as superposition and entanglement occur. Quantum physics has been used to explain many natural phenomena, including the behavior of light, the structure of atoms, and the properties of materials.

In quantum physics, everything is made of energy, including matter. Energy is a fundamental property of the universe, and it comes in different forms, such as electromagnetic radiation and kinetic energy. Frequency is a measure of how often a wave oscillates per second. It is a crucial concept in quantum physics because everything in the universe vibrates at a certain frequency, including atoms and molecules. The frequency of a system determines its energy level and the type of interactions it can have with other systems.

Vibration is a fundamental aspect of quantum physics because everything in the universe vibrates at a certain frequency. The frequency of a system determines its energy level and the type of interactions it can have with other systems. Vibrations can be measured in different ways, such as by the wavelength of a wave or the number of oscillations per second. In quantum physics, the vibration of particles determines their behavior and properties, such as their position and momentum.

The Law of Attraction and Quantum Physics

The Law of Attraction and quantum physics share a deep connection that may not be immediately apparent. However, both are based on the fundamental principles of energy, vibration, and consciousness.

Quantum physics is the study of the behavior of matter and energy on a subatomic level. At this level, the traditional laws of physics that govern the macro world no longer apply. Instead, everything is subject to the principles of quantum mechanics, which describe the behavior of particles at the smallest scales.

The Law of Attraction, on the other hand, is a principle that states that we attract into our lives whatever we focus on and believe in. It is based on the idea that we are all made up of energy and that this energy vibrates at different frequencies. When we focus on positive thoughts and emotions, we raise our vibration and attract positive experiences and outcomes into our lives.

Quantum physics provides a scientific explanation for the Law of Attraction. At the subatomic level, everything is made up of energy, including our thoughts and emotions. The energy of our thoughts and emotions vibrates at different frequencies, just like everything else in the universe. This means that our thoughts and emotions can influence the energy around us and attract similar frequencies into our lives.

The relationship between energy and matter is another important aspect of quantum physics that relates to the Law of Attraction. According to quantum physics, energy and matter are interchangeable. This means that our thoughts and emotions have the potential to create physical manifestations in the world around us.

For example, if you focus on positive thoughts and emotions, you may attract opportunities and experiences that align with those vibrations. On the other hand, if you focus on negative thoughts and emotions, you may attract experiences and situations that reflect those vibrations.

Understanding the connection between the Law of Attraction and quantum physics can help you apply the principles of manifestation more effectively. By understanding the role of energy and vibration in creating your reality, you can focus your thoughts and emotions on what you truly want to attract into your life.

The Power of Intention: Setting Your Vibrational Frequency

The Law of Attraction operates on the principle that like attracts like. This means that the thoughts and emotions we put out into the universe attract similar energies and experiences back to us. Quantum physics tells us that everything in the universe is made up of energy, including our thoughts and emotions. By aligning our energy with our desired outcome, we can attract it to us with greater ease.

Every thought and emotion we have emits a specific vibrational frequency that can either attract or repel certain experiences and outcomes. Negative thoughts and emotions, such as fear, doubt, and worry, can lower our vibrational frequency and attract similar experiences to us. On the other hand, positive thoughts and emotions, such as gratitude, joy, and love, can raise our vibrational frequency and attract more positive experiences and outcomes.

To manifest our desires, we must align our energy with the frequency of what we want to attract. One way to do this is through visualization. By imagining ourselves already having what we desire and feeling the positive emotions associated with it, we raise our vibrational frequency and attract it to us. Another technique is affirmations, which are positive statements that help us reprogram our subconscious mind to align with our desires. Meditation and gratitude practices are also effective ways to raise our vibration and align with our desired outcome.

One technique for aligning our energy with our desired outcome is using affirmations. Affirmations are positive statements that reinforce the belief that we can achieve our desired outcome. For example, if we want to manifest a new job, we can repeat the affirmation, "I am successful in my new job" to ourselves daily. This technique helps us to shift our focus from negative thoughts and emotions to positive ones, which in turn raises our vibrational frequency and attracts similar frequency experiences into our lives.

Another technique is practicing gratitude. When we focus on what we are grateful for, we shift our attention away from negative thoughts and emotions, and instead focus on positive ones. Gratitude helps us to raise our vibrational frequency and attract similar frequency experiences into our lives.

The Observer Effect: How Perception Shapes Reality

The role of perception in quantum physics is a fascinating concept that highlights the power of our thoughts and beliefs in shaping our reality. According to quantum physics, the observer has an active role in shaping the reality they experience. This means that our beliefs, thoughts, and perceptions have a direct impact on the outcome of events in our lives.

Our beliefs and thoughts create a vibrational frequency that attracts similar experiences to us. If we believe that we are capable of achieving our desired outcome, our vibrational frequency will align with that belief, and we will attract situations and opportunities that support our goal.

On the other hand, if we hold limiting beliefs and negative thoughts, our vibrational frequency will align with that energy, and we will attract situations that reinforce our negative beliefs. For example, if we believe that we are not worthy of love and abundance, we will attract situations and people that reinforce that belief.

Fortunately, we can shift our limiting beliefs and perceptions to manifest our desired outcomes. One technique for doing this is through affirmations. Affirmations are positive statements that we repeat to ourselves to shift our thoughts and beliefs. For instance, if we want to manifest financial abundance, we can repeat affirmations such as "I am worthy of abundance" or "Money flows to me easily and effortlessly."

Another technique is visualization. Visualization involves creating a mental image of our desired outcome and focusing on it with positive emotions. By doing so, we create a vibrational frequency that aligns with our desired outcome and attracts it into our reality.

The Law of Attraction and Neuroscience

The Law of Attraction is closely connected to the workings of the human brain. When we focus our thoughts and emotions on a particular outcome, we create neural pathways that reinforce that particular outcome. This is because the brain is wired to seek out patterns and connections, and our thoughts and emotions are no exception.

The brain processes thoughts and emotions related to manifesting desires through various areas such as the prefrontal cortex, the amygdala, and the hippocampus. The prefrontal cortex is responsible for decision-making and planning, while the amygdala plays a role in processing emotions and the hippocampus is involved in memory formation. When we think and feel positively about our desires, these areas of the brain work together to create a neural pathway that reinforces the positive thoughts and emotions.

Positive thinking has a significant impact on brain function and overall well-being. Studies have shown that positive thinking can increase the production of feel-good hormones such as dopamine and serotonin, which in turn can lead to improved mood, reduced stress, and better overall health. By focusing our thoughts and emotions on positive outcomes, we can rewire our brain to create new patterns and connections that support our desires.

CHAPTER XVI

Attracting Success and Achievement: Cultivating a Winning Mindset

Understanding the Psychology of Success and Achievement

Having a fixed mindset means believing that our abilities and qualities are predetermined and cannot be changed. On the other hand, a growth mindset is the belief that our abilities and qualities can be developed through effort and perseverance. People with a fixed mindset often avoid challenges and may give up easily, while those with a growth mindset embrace challenges and are more likely to persist in the face of setbacks.

Our mindset has a significant impact on our success and achievement. Research shows that those with a growth mindset are more likely to achieve their goals, learn from their failures, and persist in the face of challenges. In contrast, those with a fixed mindset may feel stuck or limited in their abilities, leading to a lack of progress and achievement.

Belief is a powerful force that can greatly impact our ability to achieve our goals. When we believe in ourselves and our abilities, we are more likely to take action, persist in the face of challenges, and ultimately achieve success. Conversely, when we doubt ourselves or have limiting beliefs, we may hold ourselves back from taking risks or pursuing our goals.

Overall, cultivating a growth mindset and developing a strong sense of belief in ourselves and our abilities can help us achieve greater success and achievement in all areas of life.

Strategies for Developing a Winning Mindset

A growth mindset is a belief that one's abilities can be developed through dedication, effort, and hard work. Cultivating a growth mindset involves adopting a positive attitude towards challenges, failures, and feedback. Some techniques for cultivating a growth mindset include:

- Embracing challenges as opportunities for growth and learning.
- Focusing on the process rather than the outcome.
- Viewing mistakes and failures as part of the learning process.
- Seeking feedback and using it to improve.
- Believing that abilities and talents can be developed through dedication and hard work.

Self-doubt and negative self-talk can be major obstacles to achieving success and achieving goals. Overcoming these obstacles involves recognizing and challenging negative thoughts and beliefs. Some techniques for overcoming self-doubt and negative self-talk include:

- Practicing self-compassion and self-kindness.
- Challenging negative thoughts and beliefs with evidence and positive affirmations.
- Replacing negative self-talk with positive self-talk.
- Surrounding yourself with positive and supportive people.
- Focusing on strengths and accomplishments rather than weaknesses and failures.

Visualization and positive affirmations are powerful tools for building confidence, motivation, and a positive mindset. Visualization involves imagining a desired outcome or goal in vivid detail, while positive affirmations involve repeating positive statements about oneself. Some ways in which visualization and positive affirmations can be used to build confidence and motivation include:

- Visualizing success and achievement in a specific area of life.
- Using positive affirmations to reinforce positive beliefs and thoughts.
- Using visualization and positive affirmations to overcome fears and self-doubt.
- Practicing visualization and positive affirmations regularly to strengthen the mindset.

Overall, cultivating a growth mindset, overcoming self-doubt and negative self-talk, and using visualization and positive affirmations are key to building a winning mindset and achieving success and achievement. It takes practice, dedication, and persistence to develop these skills, but the benefits are well worth it.

Goal Setting and Planning for Success

Setting realistic and achievable goals is an essential aspect of cultivating a winning mindset. It's important to set goals that challenge you while also being attainable. This helps to build confidence and motivation as you make progress towards your desired outcome. When setting goals, it's helpful to consider the SMART framework: Specific, Measurable, Attainable, Relevant, and Time-bound. For example, if your goal is to start a business, a SMART goal might be to launch your online store within six months, with a target revenue of $10,000 in the first year.

Creating a plan of action is the next step in achieving your goals. It's important to break down your goal into manageable steps and prioritize them based on their importance and impact. This helps to prevent overwhelm and ensures that you're making progress towards your goal every day. For example, if your goal is to launch an online store, your plan of action might include researching your target market, creating a business plan, building your website, and launching a marketing campaign.

Monitoring progress is an essential part of achieving your goals. Regularly checking in on your progress helps you stay motivated and adjust your strategies as needed. It's important to track both your successes and your failures, as they both offer valuable lessons and insights. For example, if your goal is to launch an online store, you might track your progress by monitoring your website traffic, sales revenue, and customer feedback. This allows you to identify areas where you're excelling and areas where you need to improve.

Adjusting strategies as needed is also important in achieving your goals. Sometimes, despite our best efforts, things don't go according to plan. It's important to be flexible and willing to adjust your strategies as needed to achieve your desired outcome. For example, if your marketing campaign isn't generating the results you hoped for, you might adjust your strategy by targeting a different audience or using a different marketing channel. Being willing to pivot and adjust your strategies is an important aspect of achieving your goals and cultivating a winning mindset.

Overcoming Obstacles and Challenges

Developing resilience and perseverance are crucial components of a winning mindset. Inevitably, there will be obstacles and challenges on the road to achieving your goals, and it's important to have the mental fortitude to push through them. Resilience is the ability to bounce back from adversity, while perseverance is the willingness to keep going even when the going gets tough.

To develop resilience, it's important to practice self-care and self-compassion. This means taking time to recharge and engage in activities that bring you joy and relaxation. It also means being kind to yourself and reframing negative self-talk into positive affirmations. When faced with challenges, try to focus on what you have learned and how you can apply that knowledge moving forward.

When setbacks and failures occur, it can be tempting to give up or become discouraged. However, it's important to remember that failure is not the end, but rather an opportunity for growth. One strategy for overcoming setbacks is to reframe them as learning experiences. Ask yourself what you can learn from the situation and how you can use that knowledge to improve your approach moving forward.

Another strategy is to seek support from others. Surround yourself with people who believe in you and your goals, and who can offer encouragement and constructive feedback. Remember that setbacks and failures are a natural part of the process, and that even the most successful people have experienced them.

Learning from mistakes is crucial to achieving success. It's important to take responsibility for your mistakes and use them as opportunities for growth. When you make a mistake, reflect on what went wrong and what you could have done differently. Use that knowledge to adjust your strategies and improve your approach in the future. Remember that mistakes do not define you, but rather provide valuable lessons that can help you achieve your goals.

The Importance of Mindful Success

The pursuit of success and achievement can sometimes feel overwhelming, leading to burnout and a lack of fulfillment. However, cultivating mindfulness can help you approach your goals with more balance and perspective, leading to greater success and satisfaction.

Mindfulness involves being present in the moment and fully engaged in your thoughts, feelings, and surroundings. When it comes to achieving success, mindfulness can help you stay focused on the present moment and avoid becoming too attached to future outcomes. By staying present and aware, you can more easily adapt to changing circumstances and overcome obstacles.

Along with mindfulness, it's important to cultivate a balanced approach to success and achievement. This means focusing not only on professional or financial success, but also on personal growth, relationships, and overall well-being. When you take a holistic approach to success, you can avoid burnout and maintain a sense of fulfillment and purpose.

Gratitude and reflection are also important components of sustained success. Practicing gratitude involves recognizing and appreciating the positive aspects of your life, even amidst challenges and setbacks. By cultivating a sense of gratitude, you can maintain a positive mindset and perspective, which can help you overcome obstacles and stay motivated.

Reflection involves taking time to evaluate your progress, celebrate successes, and learn from mistakes. By reflecting on your experiences, you can identify patterns and areas for improvement, and adjust your strategies accordingly. Reflection also helps you stay connected to your values and purpose, which can help you stay motivated and focused on your goals.

For example, if you're pursuing a challenging career goal, practicing mindfulness can help you stay focused and avoid becoming overwhelmed by stress and pressure. Cultivating a balanced approach to success can involve setting goals not only related to work, but also to relationships, health, and personal growth. Practicing gratitude can involve recognizing the support and resources you have, and reflecting on your progress can help you identify areas for improvement and stay motivated to continue pursuing your goals.

In summary, mindfulness, balance, gratitude, and reflection can all play important roles in achieving success and fulfillment. By cultivating these practices, you can approach your goals with greater awareness, resilience, and perspective, leading to greater overall success and satisfaction.

CHAPTER XVII

Overcoming Self-Doubt and Fear: Building Confidence and Resilience

Understanding the root causes of self-doubt and fear

Our past experiences, especially negative ones, can leave a lasting impact on our self-perception and beliefs about ourselves. Childhood experiences, traumatic events, and negative feedback from others can all contribute to self-doubt and fear. For example, if someone was constantly told they were not good enough growing up, they may struggle with self-doubt and fear of failure as an adult. It's important to explore and understand how our past experiences may be influencing our current thought patterns and behaviors.

Societal pressures and expectations can also have a significant impact on our self-perception and beliefs about ourselves. We are often bombarded with messages about what success and happiness look like, and it can be challenging to separate our own desires and values from those imposed upon us by society. For example, societal expectations around beauty and body image can contribute to feelings of inadequacy and self-doubt for many individuals. It's important to critically examine these messages and determine whether they align with our own values and beliefs.

Self-doubt and fear often stem from certain thought patterns and beliefs that we hold about ourselves and our abilities. These can include beliefs such as "I'm not good enough" or "I'll never be able to succeed." It's important to identify these thought patterns and challenge them with evidence to the contrary. For example, if someone is struggling with the belief that they are not good enough, they can look for evidence in their past experiences where they have succeeded or accomplished something they are proud of.

Techniques for building self-confidence

Developing a positive self-image through affirmations and visualization: One of the ways to overcome self-doubt and build confidence is by developing a positive self-image. Positive affirmations and visualization techniques can help in achieving this. Affirmations are positive statements that one can repeat to themselves to reinforce positive beliefs about themselves. Visualization is the process of creating a mental image of oneself achieving their goals and aspirations. By consistently practicing positive affirmations and visualization, one can start to believe in themselves and their abilities.

Setting achievable goals and celebrating successes along the way: Another way to overcome self-doubt and build confidence is by setting achievable goals and celebrating successes along the way. It is important to set realistic goals that align with personal values and aspirations. By breaking down larger goals into smaller, achievable ones, one can gain momentum and confidence with each small win. Celebrating these successes along the way reinforces positive beliefs about oneself and helps to build confidence.

Practicing self-care and prioritizing personal needs: Self-care and prioritizing personal needs are important for building confidence and resilience. Taking care of oneself physically, emotionally, and mentally is crucial for overall well-being. By prioritizing personal needs, one is reinforcing positive beliefs about their self-worth and value. This can lead to increased confidence and a greater sense of control over one's life.

Surrounding oneself with positive and supportive people: The people we surround ourselves with can have a significant impact on our self-perception and confidence levels. Surrounding oneself with positive and supportive people who believe in us and our abilities can help to reinforce positive beliefs and build confidence. On the other hand, being around negative and unsupportive people can contribute to self-doubt and insecurity. It is important to recognize and limit interactions with people who have a negative impact on our self-perception.

Strategies for overcoming fear

Facing fears can be a daunting task, but it's essential for building confidence and resilience. Exposure therapy and gradual desensitization are techniques that involve facing fears in a controlled and safe environment. For example, someone with a fear of heights may start by looking at pictures of tall buildings, then gradually work up to standing on a high balcony.

Challenging negative thoughts is also an important step in overcoming self-doubt and fear. By recognizing and questioning negative self-talk, it's possible to reframe those thoughts in a more positive light. For example, instead of thinking "I'm not good enough," one could reframe that thought as "I'm capable and have accomplished many things."

Developing coping mechanisms and relaxation techniques can also be helpful in managing anxiety. Deep breathing, meditation, and visualization exercises can all help to calm the mind and body.

In some cases, seeking professional help may be necessary. Therapists can provide additional tools and techniques for managing anxiety and overcoming self-doubt and fear. They can also provide a safe and supportive space to explore and work through underlying issues that may be contributing to these feelings.

Ultimately, building confidence and resilience requires a commitment to facing fears and challenging negative thoughts. By developing coping mechanisms, seeking support, and celebrating successes along the way, it's possible to overcome self-doubt and fear and achieve personal growth and fulfillment.

Building resilience in the face of setbacks

Failure is often seen as a negative experience, but it can be a valuable learning opportunity. Instead of dwelling on the negative aspects of failure, it's important to approach it with a growth mindset. This means seeing failure as a chance to learn and improve, rather than a reflection of your worth as a person.

A growth mindset is the belief that you can develop your skills and abilities through hard work and dedication. This mindset embraces challenges and sees them as opportunities for growth and learning, rather than something to be avoided.

Negative self-talk can be a major contributor to self-doubt and fear. It's important to practice self-compassion and reframe negative self-talk into positive affirmations. Instead of putting yourself down, try to focus on your strengths and accomplishments.

Having a support network of positive and supportive people can be invaluable in overcoming self-doubt and fear. This can include friends, family, mentors, or even a therapist or coach. Don't be afraid to seek help when needed and reach out to your support network for encouragement and guidance.

Maintaining confidence and resilience in the long-term

Cultivating a positive and growth-oriented mindset is crucial in overcoming self-doubt and achieving success. This involves focusing on personal growth and development rather than comparing oneself to others or feeling stuck in limitations. By adopting a growth mindset, individuals can approach challenges with a sense of optimism and a belief in their ability to learn and improve. For example, instead of viewing a setback as a failure, someone with a growth mindset may view it as an opportunity to learn and grow from the experience.

Practicing mindfulness and staying present in the moment can help individuals overcome self-doubt and fear by reducing anxiety and promoting a sense of calm. Mindfulness techniques such as deep breathing, meditation, and yoga can help individuals become more aware of their thoughts and emotions, allowing them to better manage negative self-talk and self-doubt.

Reflecting on successes and expressing gratitude for progress made is important for maintaining a positive outlook and building self-confidence. By acknowledging past accomplishments and expressing gratitude for positive aspects of one's life, individuals can focus on the positive rather than getting stuck in self-doubt or negative thought patterns. For example, someone who recently overcame a fear of public speaking may reflect on their progress and express gratitude for the opportunity to learn and grow from the experience.

Continuing to set goals and work towards personal growth and fulfillment is key in maintaining a positive and growth-oriented mindset. By setting achievable goals and working towards them consistently, individuals can build confidence in their ability to achieve success and overcome self-doubt. It is important to remember that personal growth is a lifelong journey, and setbacks and challenges are a natural part of the process.

Overall, cultivating a positive and growth-oriented mindset requires consistent effort and a willingness to challenge oneself. By practicing mindfulness, reflecting on successes, and continuing to set goals, individuals can overcome self-doubt and achieve success and fulfillment in their personal and professional lives.

CHAPTER XVIII

Manifesting Your Dream Career: Aligning Your Passion with Your Professional Life

Discovering Your Passion and Purpose

To manifest your dream career, the first step is to identify your interests, values, and strengths. Take some time to reflect on what you enjoy doing, what values are important to you, and what skills and talents you possess. Make a list of these things and consider how they can be applied in a professional context. For example, if you enjoy writing, value creativity, and possess strong communication skills, you may consider pursuing a career in content creation or marketing. By identifying your passions and aligning them with potential career paths, you are taking a step towards creating a fulfilling professional life.

Once you have identified your passions, it's important to understand how they can align with potential career paths. Research different industries and job roles to see how your interests, values, and strengths can be applied. You can also seek out informational interviews or job shadowing opportunities to get a better sense of what a particular career entails. For example, if you are passionate about environmental conservation, you may consider a career in sustainability consulting, wildlife management, or environmental policy. By understanding how your passions can align with potential career paths, you can begin to narrow down your options and focus on pursuing opportunities that are truly meaningful to you.

To truly manifest your dream career, it's important to find meaning and purpose in your work. This means identifying how your professional pursuits align with your personal values and goals. You can do this by reflecting on what you hope to achieve through your career, such as making a positive impact on your community or pursuing a particular cause. By finding purpose and meaning in your work, you are more likely to feel fulfilled and motivated to succeed in your chosen career path.

Overcoming Limiting Beliefs and Self-Doubt

When it comes to manifesting your dream career, it's important to address any negative beliefs or self-talk that may be holding you back. These can be limiting beliefs like "I'm not good enough" or "I'll never be able to make a living doing what I love." It's natural to have these thoughts, but it's important not to let them hold you back from pursuing your passions.

One way to address these negative beliefs is to identify them and challenge them. Ask yourself if these beliefs are really true, or if they are just a reflection of your fears and insecurities. You can also reframe these beliefs into more positive and empowering statements. For example, instead of thinking "I'll never be able to make a living doing what I love," you can reframe it as "I have the skills and talent to pursue my passions and create a successful career."

Building confidence and self-worth is also key to pursuing your dreams. This can involve practicing self-care, setting boundaries, and celebrating your successes along the way. It's important to remember that pursuing your passions may not always be easy, but it's worth it to invest in yourself and your happiness.

For example, let's say someone has always dreamed of being a writer, but has been held back by the belief that they are not talented enough. They can challenge this belief by reminding themselves of their past successes, such as receiving positive feedback on a school paper or receiving recognition for their writing on social media. They can also reframe their negative beliefs by telling themselves "I have a unique perspective and voice that is valuable in the writing world." By building their confidence and self-worth, they can take steps towards pursuing their dream career as a writer.

Setting Clear and Attainable Career Goals

Creating a vision for your dream career can be a daunting task, but it is an essential step in manifesting it into reality. You must first identify your core values, passions, and interests to align them with a potential career path. Once you have identified your dream career, it's time to create a vision for what that looks like in your life. Take some time to envision yourself in your dream job, see the environment you work in, visualize the people you interact with and feel the emotions you'd experience in that role. The more specific and detailed your vision, the more it will help you stay motivated and focused on your goal.

Once you have a clear vision of your dream career, the next step is to set specific, measurable goals to achieve it. These goals should be broken down into short-term and long-term goals that are specific, achievable, and realistic. For example, if you want to become a successful entrepreneur, a short-term goal could be to research and identify potential business ideas, while a long-term goal could be to launch your first successful product or service within a year.

Identifying the skills and experiences needed to reach your goals is another crucial step in manifesting your dream career. Research the qualifications, experience, and skills needed for your desired career and identify any gaps in your own knowledge or experience. Take the time to learn and develop the necessary skills and gain relevant experience through internships, volunteering, or side projects.

Breaking down larger goals into smaller, achievable steps is a vital aspect of achieving your dream career. When setting your goals, break them down into smaller, more manageable tasks. This approach will help you stay motivated and focused on your progress, as well as give you a sense of accomplishment when you complete each step.

Taking Action and Embracing Opportunities

Developing a plan of action and taking consistent steps towards your career goals is crucial for manifesting your dream career. Without a plan, it can be easy to feel overwhelmed and directionless. Start by breaking down your larger goals into smaller, more manageable steps. For example, if your dream career is to become a published author, your smaller goals could be to write a certain number of pages per day or to attend a writing workshop to improve your skills.

Embracing opportunities to gain new experiences and skills, even if they are outside your comfort zone, is essential for personal and professional growth. It can be easy to stay within our comfort zones and avoid taking risks, but taking those risks can lead to incredible opportunities. For example, if you are interested in pursuing a career in finance but lack experience, consider volunteering or interning in a finance-related role to gain hands-on experience.

Networking and building relationships is also important for expanding your career opportunities. Attend industry events, join professional organizations, and reach out to mentors in your desired field. Building genuine relationships with others in your field can lead to job opportunities, collaborations, and invaluable advice.

Remember that manifesting your dream career takes time and effort. Celebrate your successes along the way, and don't be discouraged by setbacks. By staying committed to your goals and taking consistent action towards them, you can make your dream career a reality.

Manifesting Your Dream Career with the Law of Attraction

The Law of Attraction states that like attracts like, meaning that the energy you put out into the universe attracts back to you. By focusing your thoughts and energy on your desired career path, you can manifest it into your reality. This involves aligning your thoughts and beliefs with your desired outcome and taking inspired action towards your goals.

Visualization involves creating a mental image of yourself in your desired career and feeling the emotions associated with that experience. Affirmations involve repeating positive statements to yourself about your abilities and the success you will achieve. Gratitude involves expressing appreciation for what you already have and the opportunities that come your way. By consistently using these techniques, you can create a positive mindset and attract the career you desire.

It is important to trust that the universe has a plan for you and that the right opportunities will present themselves at the right time. This means letting go of any limiting beliefs or negative thoughts that may be blocking your success. By surrendering control and having faith in the process, you can allow opportunities to flow into your life effortlessly

CHAPTER XIX

Attracting Positive Energy and People: Surrounding Yourself with Optimism and Encouragement

Understanding the power of positive energy and how it influences our experiences

Everything in the universe is made up of energy, including our thoughts and emotions. When we think positive thoughts, we emit positive energy, which attracts positive experiences and people into our lives. On the other hand, negative thoughts and emotions emit negative energy, which can block our ability to attract positive things. It is essential to understand the power of energy and how it impacts our lives to attract positivity.

Negative energy can come from various sources, such as negative self-talk, fear, worry, and stress. When we hold onto negative energy, it can create a blockage that prevents positive energy from flowing into our lives. Negative energy can also attract negative experiences and people into our lives, making it difficult to manifest positivity. It is crucial to identify and release negative energy to attract positivity and abundance.

There are several ways to shift our energy to attract positivity, including mindfulness, meditation, visualization, and gratitude. Mindfulness and meditation help to quiet the mind, release negative thoughts and emotions, and create space for positivity to enter. Visualization involves creating a mental image of what we desire, which helps to attract it into our lives. Gratitude helps to shift our focus onto the positive aspects of our lives and attract more positivity. By incorporating these practices into our daily lives, we can shift our energy to attract positivity and abundance.

Building a positive mindset and attracting like-minded individuals

The way we think and feel about ourselves and the world around us has a significant impact on the people and experiences we attract into our lives. If we have a negative mindset, we tend to attract negative people and experiences, while a positive mindset attracts positive people and experiences. It's important to examine our beliefs and attitudes towards ourselves and others and identify any negative thought patterns that may be holding us back.

Limiting beliefs and negative self-talk can prevent us from attracting positive people and experiences into our lives. For example, if we believe that we are not good enough or that we don't deserve love and happiness, we may subconsciously push away positive people and experiences. It's important to identify and challenge these limiting beliefs and replace them with positive affirmations that support our desired outcome.

Cultivating a positive mindset is essential for attracting positive people and experiences. Affirmations and visualization are powerful tools that can help shift our mindset and energy towards positivity. Affirmations are positive statements that we repeat to ourselves to reinforce positive beliefs and thoughts. Visualization involves picturing ourselves already having what we desire and experiencing the emotions associated with it. Other practices such as mindfulness and gratitude can also help cultivate a positive mindset.

Attracting positive people and building a supportive community can be a challenge, but there are strategies that can help. One of the most effective ways to attract like-minded individuals is by pursuing our passions and interests. When we engage in activities that we enjoy, we are more likely to meet people who share our values and beliefs. It's also important to be open and authentic when connecting with others, and to focus on building positive relationships based on mutual respect and support. Additionally, surrounding ourselves with positive influences such as inspiring books, podcasts, and mentors can help us attract more positivity and abundance into our lives.

Cultivating gratitude and appreciation to attract positivity

Understanding the power of gratitude is essential when it comes to attracting positive energy and people. Gratitude is the act of recognizing and acknowledging the good things in our lives, no matter how small they may seem. By practicing gratitude, we shift our focus from what we lack to what we have, which is an important step in attracting abundance and positivity.

There are many practices that can help cultivate gratitude, including journaling, meditation, and mindfulness exercises. By setting aside time each day to reflect on what we are grateful for, we can shift our mindset towards positivity and attract more of it into our lives. For example, taking a few minutes each day to write down three things we are grateful for can be a powerful tool in cultivating a positive mindset.

Expressing gratitude and appreciation to others is another powerful way to attract positivity and abundance. When we express gratitude, we create a ripple effect of positivity that can impact not only ourselves but those around us as well. Whether it's thanking a coworker for their help on a project or expressing appreciation for a loved one, taking the time to express gratitude can help us attract positive people and experiences into our lives.

Clearing negative energy and relationships to make room for positivity

Negative energy and toxic relationships can have a profound impact on our ability to attract positivity and abundance. It's important to identify any negative energy or relationships in our lives and take steps to release them.

One way to release negative energy is through forgiveness. Holding onto grudges or resentment can keep us stuck in negative energy, preventing us from attracting positive experiences and people. Forgiveness allows us to release that negative energy and move forward with a more positive outlook.

Another way to release negative energy is by letting go. This can involve letting go of material possessions, negative thoughts or beliefs, or even relationships that no longer serve us. Letting go can be challenging, but it can open up space for more positivity and abundance in our lives.

Setting boundaries is also crucial for eliminating toxic relationships. Sometimes we may find ourselves in relationships that drain our energy and leave us feeling depleted. It's important to recognize when this is happening and set boundaries to protect our energy and wellbeing.

Negative energy and relationships can also have a profound impact on our mental, emotional, and physical health. Studies have shown that chronic stress and negative emotions can weaken the immune system, increase inflammation in the body, and contribute to a host of health problems.

By releasing negative energy and relationships, we can improve our overall health and wellbeing, and open ourselves up to more positive experiences and relationships. The law of attraction teaches us that we attract what we put out into the universe, so it's important to cultivate positive energy and surround ourselves with positivity and encouragement.

Using the Law of Attraction to attract positive people and experiences

Understanding the principles of the Law of Attraction is essential in attracting positivity and abundance into our lives. The Law of Attraction is based on the idea that our thoughts and emotions have a magnetic energy that attracts similar energy to us. This means that we can intentionally manifest positive experiences and people by aligning our thoughts and emotions with positivity.

Visualization is a powerful tool for manifesting positivity. By creating a mental image of what we desire and holding that image in our minds, we can attract similar experiences and people to us. Affirmations, or positive statements that affirm what we desire, can also be effective in attracting positivity. By repeating affirmations regularly, we can reprogram our subconscious mind to align with positivity and abundance.

However, intention, focus, and action are also crucial in attracting positivity. It is not enough to simply think positively; we must also take action towards our goals and desires. This means setting specific and achievable goals and taking consistent steps towards them.

Positivity has a profound impact on both our personal and professional lives. In our personal lives, positivity can lead to better relationships, improved mental and emotional health, and a greater sense of fulfillment and purpose. In our professional lives, positivity can lead to greater success, improved productivity, and stronger connections with coworkers and clients.

CHAPTER XX

The Law of Attraction and Happiness: Finding Joy and Satisfaction in Life

The Science of Happiness

Happiness is a subjective experience that is influenced by many factors, including our genetics, environment, and life experiences. Positive emotions such as joy, gratitude, and contentment have been linked to a range of benefits, including improved physical health, stronger relationships, and greater resilience in the face of adversity. By understanding the science behind happiness and positive emotions, we can learn to harness the power of the Law of Attraction to cultivate greater joy and fulfillment in our lives.

There are many factors that contribute to a sense of well-being and fulfillment, including strong relationships, a sense of purpose, and a positive outlook on life. By identifying the key drivers of happiness in our own lives, we can work to align our thoughts, feelings, and actions with these factors, using the Law of Attraction to attract more positivity and satisfaction into our lives.

There are many common barriers to happiness, including negative self-talk, limiting beliefs, and social comparisons. By learning how to recognize and challenge these barriers, we can begin to shift our energy and attract more positivity into our lives. The Law of Attraction teaches us that our thoughts and beliefs shape our reality, so by focusing on positive, empowering beliefs and affirmations, we can overcome the barriers to happiness and create a more joyful, fulfilling life.

Gratitude is a powerful practice that has been shown to increase happiness, resilience, and overall well-being. By cultivating a sense of gratitude and contentment through practices such as mindfulness, journaling, and gratitude exercises, we can shift our focus away from negativity and towards the positive aspects of our lives. The Law of Attraction teaches us that we attract what we focus on, so by focusing on gratitude and positivity, we can attract more of these experiences into our lives.

Manifesting Happiness

The Law of Attraction can play a significant role in attracting happiness and satisfaction in life. Our thoughts and beliefs shape our reality, and by focusing on positive thoughts and emotions, we can manifest positive experiences in our lives. The Law of Attraction teaches us to be intentional about what we want to attract into our lives and to align our thoughts and emotions with those desires. By doing so, we can manifest our goals and dreams, including those related to happiness and fulfillment.

Setting intentions is an essential part of the Law of Attraction. It involves creating a clear picture of what we want to achieve and aligning our thoughts and actions with that vision. By focusing on positive outcomes, we can attract joy and contentment into our lives. For example, if you want to be happier in your job, you can set an intention to focus on the positive aspects of your work and visualize yourself feeling fulfilled and satisfied in your role.

Visualization, affirmations, and gratitude are powerful tools for aligning with happiness and abundance. Visualization involves creating a mental image of what you want to achieve, while affirmations are positive statements that reinforce your beliefs and desires. Practicing gratitude helps us to focus on the positive aspects of our lives and cultivate a mindset of abundance. For example, you can visualize yourself feeling happy and fulfilled in your personal relationships, repeat affirmations such as "I am worthy of love and happiness," and practice gratitude by reflecting on the things you are grateful for in your relationships.

Limiting beliefs and negative thought patterns can be significant barriers to happiness and fulfillment. These beliefs and patterns are often deeply ingrained in our subconscious mind, and we may not even be aware of them. However, by identifying them and using the Law of Attraction to overcome them, we can remove these barriers and attract more happiness and satisfaction into our lives. For example, if you have a limiting belief that you are not worthy of love, you can use affirmations to reinforce positive beliefs such as "I am worthy of love and happiness," and visualize yourself in a loving and fulfilling relationship. By doing so, you can remove the negative beliefs that are blocking your happiness and attract more positive experiences into your life.

Finding Happiness Within

Many people make the mistake of believing that external circumstances, such as wealth, success, or material possessions, are the keys to happiness. However, research suggests that true happiness comes from within and is not solely dependent on external factors. In this chapter, we will explore the concept of inner happiness and how it relates to external circumstances. We will delve into the importance of cultivating a positive mindset, building healthy relationships, and taking care of our physical and emotional well-being.

Self-love, acceptance, and compassion are crucial for cultivating inner happiness. When we love and accept ourselves, we create a solid foundation for building a life filled with joy, satisfaction, and abundance. In this section, we will explore practical techniques for cultivating self-love, such as positive self-talk, affirmations, and self-care. We will also examine the role of compassion and empathy in creating meaningful connections with others and fostering a sense of purpose and fulfillment.

Mindfulness and meditation are powerful tools for cultivating inner happiness and well-being. These practices can help us reduce stress and anxiety, increase feelings of calm and relaxation, and promote a sense of connection to the present moment. In this section, we will explore the science behind mindfulness and meditation and provide practical tips for incorporating these practices into our daily lives.

Negative emotions, such as fear, anger, and sadness, can disrupt our inner peace and block our ability to attract happiness and abundance. In this section, we will examine the impact of negative emotions on our mental and emotional well-being and explore techniques for managing them effectively. We will also delve into the principles of the Law of Attraction and how they can help us maintain a positive outlook and attract the experiences and people that bring us joy and satisfaction.

Example: If you are feeling stressed or anxious, you can use the Law of Attraction to shift your focus towards positivity. Start by setting an intention to cultivate feelings of peace and calm. Then, use visualization or affirmations to imagine yourself in a peaceful and relaxing environment. Finally, take action to create that environment, such as listening to calming music, practicing yoga or meditation, or taking a walk in nature. By aligning your thoughts, emotions, and actions with positivity, you can attract more joy and satisfaction into your life.

The Power of Connection

Our social connections and relationships have a profound impact on our happiness and overall sense of well-being. Research has shown that people with strong social connections are more likely to experience happiness, better health, and a longer lifespan. When we surround ourselves with positive, supportive people, we are more likely to experience happiness and fulfillment. On the other hand, toxic relationships can be draining and negatively impact our mental and physical health.

The Law of Attraction can help us to attract positive relationships and connections by aligning our energy with those of like-minded individuals. By focusing on the qualities we desire in our relationships and visualizing positive outcomes, we can draw positive people into our lives. For instance, if we desire a supportive and loving partner, we can focus on visualizing the qualities we desire in a partner and cultivate a positive, loving energy.

Building healthy relationships requires effort and a willingness to be vulnerable. We can build healthy relationships by being authentic, practicing active listening, showing empathy, and engaging in activities that bring us closer to others. We can also strengthen existing connections by expressing gratitude, showing appreciation, and staying present in the moment.

Toxic relationships can be harmful to our well-being, and it's important to identify and overcome them using the Law of Attraction. We can start by recognizing the patterns of behavior that are causing harm in the relationship and setting healthy boundaries. By focusing on our own energy and desires, we can detach from the negative energy of the toxic relationship and draw positive experiences and people into our lives. For example, we can focus on visualizing a peaceful and harmonious life without the negative influence of a toxic relationship.

Overall, the Law of Attraction can help us attract positive relationships and connections, build healthy relationships, and overcome toxic ones. By focusing on positive energy, gratitude, and mindfulness, we can cultivate a happier and more fulfilling life.

Cultivating a Life of Purpose

When we have a sense of purpose and meaning in life, it can bring us a deep sense of fulfillment and satisfaction. Studies have shown that having a sense of purpose can lead to improved mental and physical health, increased resilience, and greater overall life satisfaction. However, it can be challenging to identify our purpose, especially if we've been stuck in a routine or feeling unfulfilled for a long time.

One way to uncover our purpose is to explore our personal values and passions. What are the things that matter most to us? What brings us joy and fulfillment? By reflecting on these questions, we can start to create a vision for a life that aligns with our deepest values and passions. For example, if we value creativity, we might explore ways to incorporate more creative pursuits into our daily lives.

Once we've identified our purpose and created a vision for a fulfilling life, the Law of Attraction can help us align with abundance and attract the people and experiences that support our goals. By focusing our thoughts and emotions on our vision and taking inspired action towards our goals, we can attract the resources and opportunities we need to fulfill our purpose.

Of course, taking action towards a purposeful life is not always easy. We may encounter obstacles and setbacks along the way. However, by staying focused on our vision and using the Law of Attraction to attract positive energy and support, we can overcome challenges and move towards our goals with greater ease and joy.

One strategy for taking action towards a purposeful life is to break down our goals into small, manageable steps. By taking action towards our goals each day, even if they are small steps, we build momentum and create a sense of progress. We can also seek out support and guidance from like-minded individuals who share our values and passions.

CHAPTER XXI

Mindfulness and Meditation: Enhancing Your Manifestation Practice through Awareness and Presence.

Understanding the Power of Mindfulness and Meditation in the Manifestation Process

Mindfulness and meditation have been studied extensively by scientists and researchers, and their benefits have been documented in numerous studies. For example, research has shown that mindfulness and meditation can reduce stress, anxiety, and depression, while also improving overall well-being and cognitive function. Additionally, mindfulness and meditation can increase brain activity in areas associated with positive emotions and social awareness, which can enhance our ability to attract positivity and abundance.

present-moment awareness is a key component of mindfulness and meditation, and it can also play a crucial role in manifesting positive outcomes through the Law of Attraction. By focusing our attention on the present moment, we become more attuned to our thoughts and emotions, which can help us identify negative patterns and beliefs that may be blocking our ability to manifest abundance. Additionally, being fully present in the moment allows us to appreciate the beauty and wonder of the world around us, which can help us attract positivity and abundance.

Cultivating mindfulness and meditation practices can be a powerful tool for increasing our manifestation abilities. One effective way to do this is to start by setting aside a few minutes each day to practice mindfulness and meditation. This can involve simply focusing on our breath, observing our thoughts and emotions without judgment, or visualizing positive outcomes. Over time, these practices can help us develop greater self-awareness and control over our thoughts and emotions, which can enhance our ability to manifest positive outcomes.

There are many examples of people who have successfully used mindfulness and meditation to enhance their manifestation abilities and attract positivity and abundance. For example, Olympic athletes have been known to use visualization techniques to improve their performance, while entrepreneurs often use mindfulness and meditation practices to stay focused and motivated. Additionally, many people have reported experiencing increased feelings of peace, contentment, and joy after incorporating mindfulness and meditation into their daily lives. By practicing these techniques consistently, we can also experience similar benefits and enhance our ability to manifest positive outcomes.

Exploring Mindfulness Techniques to Enhance Manifestation

Mindfulness is the practice of being fully present and engaged in the current moment without judgment. It involves paying attention to the thoughts, feelings, and physical sensations that arise in the present moment. Mindfulness techniques such as breathwork and body awareness can help increase self-awareness and improve manifestation skills.

Breathwork is a mindfulness technique that involves intentionally regulating your breathing. By focusing on your breath and slowing it down, you can calm your mind and reduce stress, anxiety, and negative thoughts. This can help you align your energy with positive outcomes and enhance your ability to manifest what you desire.

Body awareness is another mindfulness technique that involves paying attention to the sensations in your body. This can help you identify areas of tension or discomfort and release them through physical movement or relaxation techniques. By improving your connection with your body, you can increase your overall sense of well-being and improve your manifestation abilities.

To cultivate mindfulness practices for manifestation, it's important to develop a daily routine. This can include setting aside a few minutes each day for breathwork or body awareness exercises, as well as integrating mindfulness into your daily activities. For example, you can practice mindful eating by savoring each bite and paying attention to the flavors and textures.

Real-life examples of how mindfulness techniques have helped others manifest their desires are abundant. For instance, Oprah Winfrey has been a long-time advocate for mindfulness and meditation, and attributes much of her success to these practices. In her book "The Path Made Clear," she shares how mindfulness helps her stay focused on her goals and align her energy with positive outcomes.

Another example is the popular author and speaker, Gabby Bernstein, who has incorporated mindfulness techniques into her daily routine and credits them with helping her overcome anxiety and manifest her desires. In her book "The Universe Has Your Back," she shares how she uses breathwork and body awareness to release limiting beliefs and align with her true desires.

By incorporating mindfulness techniques into your manifestation practice, you can increase your self-awareness, reduce stress and negative thoughts, and align your energy with positive outcomes. With dedication and consistency, you can improve your manifestation abilities and create the life you desire.

The Benefits of Meditation for Enhancing Manifestation

Meditation has been shown to have numerous benefits for mental and emotional well-being. It has been found to reduce stress, anxiety, depression, and improve overall mood. Meditation can also improve focus, concentration, and increase feelings of calm and relaxation. These benefits can have a positive impact on the manifestation process, as a calm and focused mind is more open to receiving and attracting positive outcomes.

Meditation can be a powerful tool in enhancing the manifestation process. By quieting the mind and focusing on positive intentions, we are better able to align our thoughts and feelings with what we want to manifest. Meditation also helps to cultivate a sense of trust and faith in the process, allowing us to release any doubts or fears that may be blocking our manifestation abilities.

To cultivate a meditation practice, it is important to set aside time each day for meditation. This can be as little as 5-10 minutes, to begin with, and gradually increase over time. Find a quiet and comfortable space where you can sit comfortably and focus on your breath. There are many different types of meditation, so experiment with different techniques to find what works best for you. Guided meditations, chanting, or visualization can also be helpful in enhancing manifestation abilities.

There are countless examples of individuals who have used meditation to enhance their manifestation abilities and attract positive outcomes into their lives. Oprah Winfrey, for example, has been a long-time advocate for meditation and has attributed much of her success to her daily meditation practice. Actress Jennifer Aniston has also spoken about how meditation has helped her to stay focused and positive in her personal and professional life. By incorporating meditation into your manifestation practice, you can join the ranks of these successful individuals who have harnessed the power of meditation to manifest their desires.

Mindfulness and Meditation for Overcoming Limiting Beliefs and Negative Thoughts

Identifying limiting beliefs and negative thought patterns is an essential step towards manifesting our desires. Many of us hold negative beliefs about ourselves, others, and the world around us, which can act as barriers to our manifestation abilities. For example, a common limiting belief is, "I'm not good enough." This belief can create feelings of inadequacy and doubt, which can prevent us from taking action towards our goals.

One of the ways to overcome limiting beliefs and negative thought patterns is through mindfulness and meditation. These practices help us become more aware of our thoughts and emotions, and can help us identify patterns that may be holding us back. For example, through mindfulness meditation, we can observe our thoughts and emotions without judgment, and begin to notice when negative beliefs arise.

Once we've identified limiting beliefs and negative thought patterns, we can use mindfulness and meditation techniques to release them. One such technique is called "noting." When we notice a negative thought or belief arising during our meditation practice, we can simply note it as "thinking" and let it go. By acknowledging these thoughts and releasing them, we can begin to cultivate a more positive mindset.

Developing a regular mindfulness and meditation practice can also help us cultivate a more positive mindset overall. By focusing on the present moment and letting go of negative thoughts and emotions, we can begin to see the world around us in a more positive light. This positive mindset can help us attract more positive experiences into our lives.

Real-life examples of how mindfulness and meditation have helped others overcome limiting beliefs and negative thought patterns include individuals who have used these practices to manage anxiety and depression, improve self-esteem, and overcome trauma. For example, a study published in the Journal of Traumatic Stress found that mindfulness-based stress reduction was effective in reducing symptoms of post-traumatic stress disorder (PTSD) in veterans. Another study published in the Journal of Happiness Studies found that mindfulness meditation was effective in improving self-esteem and reducing symptoms of depression.

Combining Mindfulness, Meditation, and Visualization Techniques for Powerful Manifestation

Mindfulness, meditation, and visualization techniques are powerful tools that work together to help individuals enhance their manifestation abilities. Mindfulness helps to create present-moment awareness, meditation helps to quiet the mind and focus on positive intentions, and visualization helps to create a clear mental picture of what one desires.

Present-moment awareness is crucial in manifesting positive outcomes because it helps individuals to be fully present and focused on the moment. By being mindful of their thoughts and emotions, individuals can identify negative patterns and limiting beliefs that may be blocking their manifestation abilities. This awareness also allows individuals to identify and seize opportunities that may arise.

Combining mindfulness, meditation, and visualization practices can help individuals maximize their manifestation potential. To do this, one should begin with mindfulness techniques to create present-moment awareness, followed by meditation to quiet the mind and focus on positive intentions, and finally visualization to create a clear mental picture of the desired outcome. By combining these practices, individuals can increase their ability to manifest their desires.

Developing a daily manifestation practice that incorporates mindfulness, meditation, and visualization techniques can be a powerful way to enhance manifestation abilities. One should begin by setting aside time each day for these practices, ideally in a quiet and peaceful space. By incorporating these practices into a daily routine, individuals can cultivate a positive mindset and increase their ability to manifest their desires.

Real-life example of how combining these techniques have helped others manifest their desires

There are countless examples of how combining mindfulness, meditation, and visualization techniques have helped others manifest their desires. For example, a woman who wanted to start her own business used these techniques to visualize her success and believe in herself, eventually leading to the successful launch of her business

CHAPTER XXII

Advanced Techniques and Strategies: Taking Your Manifestation Practice to the Next Level

Quantum Manifestation

To understand how quantum physics relates to manifestation, we need to look at the concept of quantum entanglement. This principle states that particles can become entangled, meaning that they are connected in such a way that the state of one particle affects the state of the other, no matter how far apart they are. This principle can be applied to our thoughts and emotions, which are like particles in our minds. By focusing our thoughts and emotions on positive outcomes, we can entangle ourselves with the universe and create a connection that enhances manifestation.

Quantum manifestation techniques can help us overcome limitations that may be blocking our manifestation abilities. For example, if you believe that you don't have enough money to start your dream business, quantum manifestation techniques can help you overcome this limiting belief. By visualizing yourself as already having the money you need, you can create a quantum entanglement with the universe that attracts the resources you need to make your business a success.

Quantum manifestation techniques can also help us expand our possibilities beyond what we currently think is possible. By shifting our focus from what we think is achievable to what we desire, we can create a quantum entanglement with the universe that opens up new possibilities for us. For example, if you want to travel the world but think you can't afford it, quantum manifestation techniques can help you shift your focus from the limiting belief to the desire to travel. This can create a connection with the universe that attracts new opportunities to make your dream a reality.

There are many real-life examples of how quantum manifestation has helped people manifest their desires. One such example is the story of Marie Diamond, a renowned Feng Shui master and Law of Attraction expert. Marie used quantum manifestation techniques to attract success and abundance into her life. She visualized herself as already having the success and abundance she desired, and this created a quantum entanglement with the universe that attracted the resources she needed to achieve her goals.

Energy Work and the Law of Attraction

Many people believe that energy work is a new-age concept, but it has actually been around for thousands of years. In essence, energy work involves working with the energy that flows throughout the universe to manifest our desires.

One of the fundamental principles of energy work is that everything in the universe is made up of energy, including our thoughts and emotions. This energy can either be positive or negative, and our energy vibrations attract similar energies to us.

To attract positive energy, we need to understand how to work with the universal energy that surrounds us. This involves becoming aware of our thoughts and emotions and learning how to align them with our desires. When we are in alignment with the energy of our desires, we attract more of it into our lives.

There are several energy work techniques that can help us to do this, including visualization, affirmations, and gratitude. Visualization involves creating a mental image of what we want to manifest, while affirmations involve repeating positive statements to ourselves. Gratitude involves focusing on the things we are grateful for, which raises our energy vibration and attracts more positive energy.

Developing a daily energy work practice is key to enhancing our manifestation abilities. This can involve setting aside time each day to focus on our desires and perform energy work techniques. The more consistent we are in our energy work practice, the more powerful our manifestation abilities become.

There are many real-life examples of how energy work has helped others manifest their desires. For instance, people who have used visualization techniques to imagine themselves in their desired career have found themselves being offered the job. Others who have used gratitude practices have attracted abundance and positivity into their lives.

One famous example of the power of energy work is the story of Jim Carrey. Before becoming famous, Carrey wrote himself a check for $10 million, which he dated five years into the future. He carried the check around with him everywhere he went, visualizing himself as a successful actor. Five years later, he received a $10 million paycheck for his role in Dumb and Dumber.

Conscious Creation

Successful manifestors share common traits such as clarity of intention, unwavering belief in their ability to manifest their desires, and a deep sense of gratitude for what they have in their lives. They are also able to maintain a positive mindset, focus on the present moment, and stay persistent in the face of challenges. In order to enhance your manifestation abilities, it is important to understand and cultivate these qualities.

Cultivating the qualities of successful manifestors requires a shift in mindset and the development of new habits. One effective way to start is by setting clear intentions and focusing on them daily. This can be done through visualization, affirmations, or journaling. It is also important to let go of limiting beliefs and negative self-talk, and replace them with positive, empowering thoughts.

A daily practice of conscious creation involves aligning your thoughts, emotions, and actions with your desires in a deliberate and intentional way. This can include practices such as gratitude, visualization, affirmations, and meditation. It is important to stay focused on your desired outcomes, while also being open to unexpected opportunities that may arise.

There are countless examples of people who have used the power of conscious creation to manifest their desires. One such example is Oprah Winfrey, who attributes her success to her ability to manifest her dreams through visualization and positive affirmations.

The Power of Gratitude

Gratitude is a powerful emotion that can have a significant impact on manifestation. When we express gratitude, we are acknowledging the abundance and blessings in our lives, which can attract even more positivity into our experiences.

Research has shown that gratitude can improve overall well-being, increase happiness, and reduce stress and anxiety. In the context of manifestation, gratitude helps us focus on what we already have and feel thankful for it, rather than obsessing over what we lack.

To cultivate a daily gratitude practice, start by setting aside a few minutes each day to reflect on the things you are grateful for. This can be done in the morning, at night, or any time throughout the day that works best for you. You can use a journal to write down your gratitude list, or simply take a mental note.

In addition to gratitude journaling, there are various techniques you can use to incorporate gratitude into your manifestation practice. For example, before visualizing your desired outcome, take a moment to express gratitude for it as if it has already happened. This can help you tap into the feeling of already having what you want, which can speed up the manifestation process.

Gratitude can also help you overcome obstacles and challenges that may arise during your manifestation journey. Instead of focusing on what went wrong, try shifting your perspective to what you can be grateful for in the situation. This can help you maintain a positive mindset and attract positive outcomes despite setbacks.

Intuition and the Law of Attraction

Understanding the role of intuition in manifestation is crucial to achieving success. Intuition is that inner voice, gut feeling, or sixth sense that guides you towards your desires. It is that deep knowing that cannot be logically explained but is nonetheless powerful. Intuition plays a significant role in the manifestation process, as it helps you align with the universe's energy and tap into your subconscious mind.

Cultivating your intuition requires learning to listen to your inner voice and trust your instincts. One way to do this is by quieting your mind through meditation, mindfulness, and other relaxation techniques. By creating a space of stillness within yourself, you can access your intuition more easily and allow it to guide you towards your desires.

Developing a daily practice of intuitive listening involves paying attention to your body's signals and emotions. When you tune in to your body, you can identify when something feels right or wrong, and this can help you make decisions that align with your desires. Trusting your intuition can be difficult, especially when it goes against what seems logical, but with practice, you can learn to rely on your inner voice more and more.

Real-life examples of how intuition has helped others manifest their desires are numerous. For instance, a woman may have an intuitive feeling that she should apply for a particular job, even though she doesn't meet all the qualifications. She trusts her intuition and applies, and to her surprise, she gets the job. Similarly, a man may feel a strong pull towards a particular city or country, even though he doesn't know anyone there. He follows his intuition and moves there, and he finds that he has more opportunities than he ever imagined.

By cultivating your intuition and trusting it to guide you towards your desires, you can enhance your manifestation abilities and achieve success in all areas of your life.

Printed by Libri Plureos GmbH in Hamburg,
Germany